Changing the World
is Child's Play

Inspirations for making everyday
moments with children count

Sarah Amy Glensor Best

Children Change delivers education, professional development and publications for parents and caregivers to inspire and support their care of children.

First published by Ako Books in 2015.

Published by:
Sarah Amy Glensor Best - Children Change
www.childrenchange.co.nz
+64 21 1174 899
sarah@childrenchange.co.nz

A catalogue record for the original version of this book is available from the National Library of New Zealand.

ISBN: 978-0-9941142-1-1

Design and layout: Claude88Design
Second edition updates and conversion: Wakefields Digital
Printed in New Zealand by: Wakefields Digital – www.wakefields.co.nz

This book is dedicated to my father who has retained play as a priority
throughout his life of tireless support for the community

Whāia te iti kahurangi ki te tūohu koe me he maunga teitei.
Aim for the highest cloud so that if you miss it, you will hit a lofty mountain.

**I have a vision. A vision of all children respected as significant
human beings, with appreciation for who they are and
gratefulness for the many gifts they can offer the world.**

One of these gifts is play…

Contents

Foreword

Modern parents are the first in history to be parenting with access to the brain imaging technologies and accumulated research that give such clear feedback about what does and does not serve our children.

This can be utterly overwhelming. Knowing that early experiences have lifelong implications and that early relationships have human-forming consequences can create well intentioned parents who consistently second guess their parenting.

An antidote to this over analysis paralysis comes in the form of Sarah Amy Glensor Best's lovely book.

Written with confidence and authority, it simultaneously maintains a warm lightness of touch. Sarah's words are passionate without ever seeming bossy or didactic. At turns inspiring and entertaining, this book covers topics as broad and varied as families themselves.

"Changing the World is Child's Play" will speak intimately to the thinking parent who is looking for a playful connection with their child. Sarah Amy Glensor Best uses clear language, grounded in real life experiences and beautiful examples, to bring alive current research understanding. This book speaks to what a parent might actually do, rather than the theory alone. Better yet, the book is loaded with ideas that are no-cost, lo-fi, and screen free.

Sarah achieves the near impossible when she demystifies how to play. Play is central to all aspects of human development and while it's a simple idea, it is one of the most complicated processes of systems integration and cognitive stimulation we know of.

"Changing the World is Child's Play" manages to wrangle all this complexity into a human centred, storytelling approach that all parents can understand.

This delicious book can be devoured in one go, cover to cover. However, it will be of equal value when it is served in snack sized portions. Enjoy.

Miriam McCaleb and
Nathan Mikaere-Wallis.
27th October 2014.

Miriam and Nathan share a passion for children and positive parenting. They each have nationwide and international reputations as writers, speakers and educators. Nathan works as a consultant in Australia and New Zealand, he is a trustee and kaiako (educator) for Brainwave Trust, sits on many boards and has been a lecturer at Canterbury University. Miriam is currently focusing on being mama to two children. She has also been a university lecturer in New Zealand and the United States, a Brainwave South Island founding kaiako and regularly writes for magazines around Aotearoa. Her website is worth a peek: www.baby.geek.nz.

Introduction

I really believe that everyday experiences and interactions with children are the most effective way to change the world. Imagine if every adult realised that each moment spent with children counted.

Imagine if they realised that each of these moments had the potential to make a difference in our world. How would our world look and feel? Imagine how it would grow.

Looking back, it was with this in mind that the first seeds for this book were sown. As I grew into my role as a parent and progressed through Playcentre with my children, it began to sink in just how important our time together is, doing real life, everyday things. I also recognised how much I was learning from my children and, in turn, how much I was influencing their decisions in life. This understanding was reinforced through my training in the Playcentre Education Diploma in Early Childhood and Adult Education. My understanding was further deepened as I embarked on the journey to become a kaiako (educator) for Brainwave Trust Aotearoa.

During these wonder-full journeys – parenting, Playcentre and Brainwave Trust – I realised I'd amassed a wealth of experience and knowledge about human development. I also realised that everyone could have this. But sometimes it was out of reach due to the pressures of modern day living or simply lack of recognition of its importance. It was here that I felt a real desire to share this wealth.

I began to consider how 'child's play' has become associated in many societies with being something very easily done, trivial, of little importance, somewhat irrelevant and even being without purpose. Nature, however, has a clear purpose for 'child's play'. Play allows children to adapt and grow in their environment.

As such, real life experiences – as opposed to contrived, play experiences – are important. As living, interdependent beings, children relate to experiences linking them to their own bodies; to other people and to the wider natural world. This realisation initiated a broadening of my definition of play.

Through neuroscience (science dealing with the structure and function of the brain), we now know that the experiences children have in their early years – particularly those experiences with adults with whom they have a primary relationship – play a crucial role in the creation of wiring; the laying down of the super highways; the foundations of their brains. The ways in which they are 'wired up' defines how children view themselves other people and the world around them. This remains throughout their lives and, in turn, affects their children, and all those they interact with.

By understanding the adaptability of children's brains, we can appreciate that 'child's play' is incredibly important. Each and every experience children have has the potential to change the world. When playing, they're not just having fun – which is arguably a good enough reason to play – but also working out their way in their world. They're adapting their brains in relation to their experiences and this will impact on the future of everyone and everything they later come into contact with. This is a pretty important purpose!

The ideas and experiences offered in this book are simple and easy but not unimportant. This book invites you to discover and rediscover the importance of ordinary play in our everyday lives. By engaging in simple and real experiences – recognising their importance – we have a real chance to change the world.

I truly believe we can change the world through child's play.

How to use this book

"Changing the world is child's play" is a starting point. It is a collection of inspirations coupled with ideas to try out now! There are actions to take and reflections to make. This book suggests real life experiences and fun, loving interactions for you to have a go at with the children you spend time with. Some may be one-offs, others lifestyle-changers. These can all make a difference for you; for children and, in turn, can ripple out into the world beyond.

First steps need to be taken at the beginning of any journey. A moment missed is a moment gone. Here are a few suggestions to get going.

• Start! Make the choice to make change.

• There is no right way to choose topics or experiences. They are included in a random order in this book and many link backward and forward to other topics. Choose by randomly opening a page or work through them one-by-one. Skip those you are not interested in right now. Come back to them later. It's up to you.

• Recognise the positive impacts of – and feel affirmed for – what you are already doing.

• Challenge yourself to try something new.

• Ideally, experience these ideas with children to maximise positive differences in your world and the world as a whole. You can do these with one child or with several.

• Utilise these invitations to develop your relationships with children as a positive side effect.

• Find out what you and they enjoy most. Remember, this is a place to begin. You might try one idea or experience every week or one a day. It's up to you.

• Create other ways in which you could appreciate time spent with children.

• Experiences can be tailored to suit children of all ages and stages. For older children, find ways together to extend the play experiences. For babies and young children, bring them along for the ride by verbalising what's going on, including your inner thoughts, decisions and processes. Allow them to observe your actions and be involved whenever possible so that one day they, too, can participate fully.

Most of the experiences suggested do not require money; special equipment or even much time. They involve making a choice; having an intention to make the most out of life and being present in the moment. But most of all they involve love: love of ourselves and children; love of life and love of this very real world we all live in.

Right, let's play!

Adventures
near and far

'**A**dventure' is defined in the Oxford Dictionary as, "An unusual and exciting or daring experience." It is also defined as, "… to engage in daring or risky activity." The idea of an adventure is often relished by children. By working with them, we can make just about everything in life adventurous.

Adventures are golden learning opportunities. They offer chances to extend ourselves by a certain amount of risk taking. Adventures can be planned for just about anywhere and everywhere. "Feel the fear and do it anyway!" is the catch-cry of the bold adventurer. Children are often far better at taking this on than we adults. Why not join them? Experience the thrill of excitement; the sparkling eyes and the gleaming smiles as we push our bodies, minds and emotions further than we would usually dare. An adventure is an energiser for our spirits, more effective than any other I can think of.

So how do we go about it?

One way is to craft – or at least consider – an adventurous idea, either real life or fantasy. Doing this requires creativity and a yearning to make life count. Making an idea a real possibility can take courage and belief in ourselves as well as persistence and further creativity to make it into a workable plan. Having completed the preparation, we may choose to carry out our adventure. Or, maybe not: sometimes the planning itself is the adventure!

> One evening at dusk they were at the beach. The adult was on one side of a thick row of bushes and the children were on the other. "Where are you?" they called out to each other several times.
> The children tried to get to the other side and ended up scrambling under the bushes with much laughter, sand and scraped arms. They headed home still talking about it with twinkles in their eyes and a big hug for each other.

> "Oh my, how are we going to get all the way to your bedroom?" he asked one evening. "The lava is flowing and is getting higher all the time!" "Let's make a boat with the towel." The child responded, "What if my foot slips into the hot lava?" "I'll cast a spell so that your feet will be colder than ice. We'll be safe, Dad." They slid, scraped, giggled and hugged all the way to bed.

When we treat life as an adventure, we offer two gifts to the world: our love of life and our permission for those around us to feel the same.

However, over-planning might compromise spontaneity and this is often a feature of adventures. In any case, the steps to an adventure may not always occur discretely or linearly. The germ of an idea may hatch within our subconscious, lying dormant until an opportunity appears and the plan that was never formalised can happen: as if by magic!

Perhaps the intention to extend ourselves may have formed but not yet been consciously acknowledged. Until that one moment where we choose to say, "Sure, I'll give it a go!" quite surprising ourselves.

All that these seeds of adventure require in order to grow is an openness to taking on life's challenges in whatever forms they may appear. Then all that's left is to GO FOR IT!

Life is risky business. Creating controlled environments for children to practice having adventures will prepare them well for going out into the risky world. Letting them be brave - and grow into their bravery – may also be an adventure for you as a challenge of restraint and allowing them to learn from their own mistakes and minor hurts.

Failure to complete or even embark on the adventure as it was planned is terrific learning in itself. There are many great stories throughout history where adventures haven't quite gone to plan. The anticipation and preparation for an adventure is sometimes more satisfying and significant than what transpires throughout the actual adventure.

Experience this ...

- **Brave building.** What do you avoid? What do you secretly wish to do? What would extend your comfort zones? Consider extending yourselves by supporting each other as you venture out of your comfort zone.

- **Daring to say yes!** Notice when children request something a little daring; a little out of your comfort zones. Instead of the habitual, "No," pause and then bravely announce, "Sure, let's try it".

- **Hiding and seeking.** Offer 'hide and seek' to children who have not yet come across it or say, "Yes," when children ask you to join them. Enjoy the excitement, anticipation, problem solving, perseverance and exhilaration, all inherent in this age-old, all-ages game. Perhaps enlist the help of another 'hide and seek' savvy person to be the seeker while you and an infant or new recruit hide.

- **Make it big.** Extend the 'hide and seek' space to create a more challenging game for hiders and seekers alike. Play outside, in a park or on a side street. Count longer to allow time for more clever secret spots, or count shorter for a quick draw game with much laughter. Before beginning, discuss any safety aspects and make deals to support everyone in being responsible.

- **Seeking adventures.** Create adventures together. Note them all down. Over time plan and, importantly, go forth and adventure. Your adventure may be a sunrise swim or crawling through your garden on all fours under bushes and through puddles.

- **Life of adventure.** Recognise how much adventure is part of normal life. Speaking with a stranger; using the telephone; walking alone to school or tasting a new food. How much of normal life can be made into an adventure purely through our deciding it can be so? Seek to use creativity; bravery and physical, mental and emotional skills to work through epic adventures together, every day. Consider brushing teeth for a full and timed two minutes without pause; planning a surprise

Watch out playing 'hide and seek' with older children as they can be amazing at hiding in tricky places. Although they're often known to give themselves away with their wound up giggles and whispers.

Infants may experience you being here/not being here/being here again as an early peek-a-boo adventure before moving into toddlerhood and practicing their counting during a full blown game of 'hide and seek'.

party; walking down separate aisles in the supermarket; going on a moonlit, night-time escapade looking for hedgehogs; trying out a new bush path; dancing in the rain or jumping on a local bus without knowing its destination. How can you challenge yourselves?

- **Feel the fear and do it anyway!** When adventures in life feel too big for you or children to handle, find ways to break them down into manageable steps. Focus on achieving one of these at a time. Each step of the adventure will bring with it valuable learning.

- **Re-enactments.** Recreate famous adventure stories from your own culture and the cultures of others. Imagine the determination and faith that was rewarded by the courageous Polynesian adventurers who first paddled their waka (canoes) across the Pacific to Aotearoa!

- **Adventures after dark.** Night-time adventures can be a superb extension for adventurers ready for the next step. Try walking; swimming; playing games or spending time alone in the darkness.

- **Map it out.** Older children can practice map reading, autonomy and empowerment by being dropped off somewhere in their local community and given the opportunity to find their way home. Yes, seriously! My brother and I still remember these experiences with great joy and satisfaction. Kia ora, Mum!

I wonder ...

We don't know everything. Wondering is the process where we open ourselves to delve into the depths of our knowledge and combine this with our natural creative abilities. Children are great wonderers and questioners and an answer to each and every question is not always necessary. If all questions were answered, there would be no room for children to generate their own understandings of universal musings. "Hmmm, I wonder ...," leads children to think for themselves. This response can be used for both what we do know and what we do not know well.

Star gazing is perhaps the world's oldest hobby. Dreaming, wondering, and exploring the depths of our minds to fathom the unanswerable. What lies out there? How big is it? What are stars? And, oh dear, why are we here? "Twinkle Twinkle Little Star" hints at this human infatuation and inherent fascination with 'the beyond'. We can encourage this by directing children's thoughts out into space and providing opportunities for them to probe further into the mysteries of the universe.

'Cloud wondering' can be a delightful pastime. Consider the wider world and our own interests working in unison to create the cloud images we can fully appreciate. Staring up at the skies, we can begin with questions, perhaps starting with, "How does the world turn?" and working towards others: What is on the moon? Where is Mars? Where are we in this universe of ours? What's in the middle of the earth? How long would it take to dig a hole there? What else can we wonder about together?

I wonder why? I wonder how? I wonder ...

"Who made all of the people?" This question popped out just as he had said goodnight and was leaving the room. He thought, "How do I answer this?" Then he realised he didn't have to. I wonder how it all happened, he responded. Then he suggested, "How about you dream up how people were created?" The next morning a wonder-full description of plants and star dust and water and moon beams was given to him as a way to explain how humans came to be.

When we allow ourselves to wonder, without need for the answer, we become open to other perspectives and all that others have to offer.

Experience this ...

- **Star wondering.** Tonight, do a spot of star gazing and lunar musings letting, "I wonder ..." hang in the air as often as possible.

- **Seize opportunities** to acknowledge and discuss children's questions about space, stars, the universe, and who built the first ever house. Allow space for children's suggestions before interjecting your own knowledge.

- **Sky gazing.** Plan a time to go outside together and lay down somewhere comfortable to stare up into space. Even if no talking happens, you will share an enchanting time together.

- **What can we learn?** No one person is the fount of all knowledge. Find out more together about what you are interested in but do not know. Find out from family, friends, other people in the community, the library or – if all else fails - the internet. Fact or fantasy, it doesn't matter. It's the wondering that counts.

Creativity and learning are best sparked when children are ready to engage. Even if it's not the most opportune timing for you to utilise these moments to wonder together, consider going with it anyway. These can turn out to be magical, perfect memories to cherish.

The world is
an orchestra

A child once noted with wide-eyed delight, "Wow, the world is an orchestra". What a beautiful acknowledgement that we are surrounded by the music of life.

One of our keenest senses is hearing. Even when children don't consciously know what we are doing, they will still be readily absorbing the sounds emanating from our actions. Scraping of pans, tinkling glass, *vroom* of the vacuum cleaner, the soft scratch of pen on paper, clanging cutlery, or dull thud of wood. These are all forms of the day-to-day music making up our lives. Making music is something we do all the time, every moment.

Even when the world appears to be still, there is always some music. Perhaps only the rhythmic soft sighs of our breath inhaling and exhaling or the rustling of wind through leaves. We are surrounded by music. Appreciating and harnessing this in children's play (their daily work) supports the development of their expression and musical potential.

Children have wonderful talents for making music, and, as with movement, language and complex mathematical problem-solving, there are stages that must be worked through in order to achieve their full music-making potential.

Voice is the first instrument, closely followed by utilising increased body control to clap and slap body parts together. Grasping objects then shaking them or banging them together can produce wonderfully satisfying noises for infants and toddlers – their faces a picture of delight as they discover further evidence of the principle of cause and effect.

Progressing through childhood, the creative potential and musical execution can further increase to a more formal appreciation of music such as learning to play an instrument. Other than this however, support in the forms of opportunity, encouragement and a suitable environment in which to practice, is all that we need provide.

A father and son were cooking together. The boy was stirring, Dad was scooping. Suddenly the boy tapped the bowl with the spoon, three times. Dad answered the beats by thrice banging the measuring cup on the bench. Another three sounded from the boy and again the father answered. Within moments they were rocking out their cooking beats together, while beaming at each other. What music they were making!

> Music, in all its many forms, is a gift to the world, allowing us to express our life, love, and longing to make a difference.

Experience this ...

- **A world of music.** Notice the music in nature, our bodies and our daily tasks. Take time to be still together, both inside and outside, and just listen, enjoying the music that is life.

- **Banding together.** Bring out pens, newspaper, shoes, boxes, old metal pots or bowls, kitchen utensils (that are no longer used), babies' treasure items, pieces of wood and other natural items – whatever you find while rummaging around together in cupboards, on shelves, out in the garden or at the beach. Lay them down and get making music together.

- **Band manager.** Support children to make their own music in and out of the house, using natural or household implements. Encourage them to let their creative spirit move them. However, bedtime may solicit a, "sounds great for first thing tomorrow," response.

- **Musical partners.** Play music together, wherever and whenever. Use your own body sounds, day-to-day items, or pretend to make music using creative imagery with your bodies.

- **Top act.** Plan, then perform a concert together including a performance plan and introductions for each piece.

- **More music.** Extend musical understanding by supporting children to draw or write up their music. Children may wish to create their own style or graphics for symbolising their symphony. Work together to create accompaniment options for backing music, singing or dancing.

Resist the urge to tell music-makers to "quieten down the racket". This can be difficult sometimes. Perhaps you or they could kindly go elsewhere during this time?

Home-made musical equipment is easy to organise and often very rewarding. You can experiment with adjusting the pitch and loudness of each 'instrument' with a little thought and ingenuity. This is a superb learning opportunity for children to see how instruments can be created and modified. Start by using different types of 'drum sticks' to create different banging sound effects.

We can (and do) make music while cooking. However it is important not to put food or kitchen equipment that we use on the floor, nor use it with non-cooking items. This is in respect of Tikanga Māori which includes considerations for the health of our bodies.

I'm so angry
I could eat the sun!

All of our feelings are valid; even anger. However, our actions – as expressions of these feelings – need to be managed so that we do not cause damage to others.

Noticing that we are feeling angry is a great place to start when managing our own anger. For many years when growing up, I didn't believe I felt anger.

A four year old girl, who had already developed a strong sense of justice, found that anger was welling up inside her regularly. Many things set her off. It may be that she hurt herself, someone did not follow her plan or that the world wasn't fair. Adults desperately wanted to scoop her up in their arms and reassure her of the goodness of the world. However, she'd scream, "GET AWAY FROM ME!" with such conviction that they did as she demanded. An adult at Playcentre realised he needed to acknowledge her intense emotion. "Wow, you are really feeling angry!" he said with big eyes and genuine conviction. She looked up at him. "Are you angry enough to eat the sun?" "Yes!" she responded passionately. He thought quickly, "Are you angry enough to run around the whole world?" "Yes!" she said, stamping her foot hard on the floor. He copied her action with equal conviction. "Whoa, are you angry enough to jump up and down on an elephant?" "Yes!" was the answer, but a little smile flashed across her face. After a few more of these outrageous suggestions for expressing anger they were both giggling away. I really get you little one and it's okay to feel angry."

At some point in my early childhood I'd decided that anger wasn't okay, so I simply denied that I was ever angry. When I finally acknowledged its existence as part of my suite of available emotions, I had to begin to affirm anger as valid and then slowly, through trial and error, work out ways to best express it – both on my own and in the presence of others. I found yelling at the top of my voice out in a large field extremely effective. This is an on-going journey for me, though it's become a more efficient one since needing to support my own children travelling this path.

Having recognised our own anger, the next step is to consider what tends to spark those feelings. For me, this usually involves frustration at things not going my way and feeling out of control. When working with children we may often feel angry about them not doing as we wish or feeling we are not in control. While lack of control is not necessarily a bad thing, it can be very stressful at the time. Expressing this feeling without blame or turning it into an attack on others is an effective way to defuse the intensity in the moment: "I'm really struggling right now!"

Lastly, during times of calm and creativity, we can create ways to acknowledge and express our angry feelings so that they do not cause those around to feel attacked by our communication or actions.

When others are expressing their anger around us, the single most helpful action we can take is to acknowledge their feelings verbally or with a nod to say, "I get that you're feeling angry". Recognising that they are feeling angry right then, let them be with that emotion rather than avoiding it, ignoring it, or getting caught up in it. Keeping calm and

We are truly free when we feel safe to express all of our emotions.

ensuring our own safety until the storm has abated is wise. It's not about us in this moment. It's about them expressing a feeling they have at that time. No matter what they are saying or trying to do to us, their actual message is, "I'm feeling angry and I need some help to express it and move on!"

Once expression and acknowledgement has occurred, a choice of action can then be taken. This may be to continue expressing the feelings further or to take some time to calm down, alone or together. Working together can be made fun.

Experience this...

- **How are you showing your anger?**
  Acknowledge and reflect on how you express your own anger. Make changes you feel necessary, one at a time.

- **Notice when you're getting distressed.** Say how you're feeling, either to yourself or out loud. Choose a method of calming down. Here are some ideas:
  - take three slow, deep belly breaths and say, "Stop," and breathe; "Calm," and breathe; "Do no harm," and breathe
  - get outside for a walk, run, dance or twirl
  - have a bath or shower
  - knead dough, whisk ingredients – get cooking

- write, draw or do crafts to both relax you and express your feelings
- do something else that helps you to move on through the anger.

- **So you get angry too.** Acknowledge children's angry feelings when they occur – what words could you give them to help them really express their distress? Let them know what you see with patience and generosity, such as, "I see you're really feeling angry!" Perhaps add, "Would you like some help to calm down?"

- **Get the anger together.** Show children you understand how they're feeling in a fun but genuine and respectful way. Use full body expressions such as stamping feet, clenching your teeth and hands, and opening your mouth and/ or eyes wide – really experiencing the anger – while finding out just how angry they really are. "Are you angry enough to eat the sun?"

- **Hmm, how did that go?** When you are both calm, discuss what the experience was like for each of you.

- **Find another way.** Offer options to help children articulate their feelings, including feelings of anger, using drawings of faces or images or colours they can point to or talk about.

- **Create an anger expression plan.** Include any of the previous suggestions along with: stomp feet, clench hands, jump up and down, stretch up tall or curl up in a ball, run around in circles or speed down the hall, either roll on the grass or lie gazing up at the sky, punch a cushion, crush a spongey ball, rip up paper, roar loudly like a lion for as long as you need, yell "I'm so angry I could jump over a volcano!", or something else outrageous.

Responsible me,
responsible you

Human beings are an interdependent species. This means we work together for our survival. We need to interact respectfully with our environment if we are to thrive on this planet. In such a high stakes team event, all of us must take responsibility for the decisions we make, the actions we take, and the feelings and reactions we choose to generate.

Appreciating that all that we think, feel, and do impacts much more broadly than simply on ourselves, we open our eyes to the possibility of change being caused through adjustments to our own behaviours and actions. We can all make a difference to our circumstances and the wider situations in the world. We need not be victims in our lives; we can be leaders of change both within ourselves and in the world around us. In the 1980s, Michael Jackson appealed to the planet to take a look at the "man in the mirror". What do we see? What can we take personal responsibility for?

Adults can model responsibility. This will encourage children to accept responsibility for their own actions. Children need opportunities to practice taking responsibility. If we want children to be responsible for the care of their things, we can demonstrate attentive and respectful treatment of both their possessions and our own. We also need to ensure they have chances to practice this responsible behaviour.

Choosing to be 'the cause' in our own lives makes a very positive difference in the world. We can

A woman lost her temper and shouted at her young son. His four year old big sister came up to Mum and said, "Mummy, you need to say sorry to him. It's not okay to shout at each other." After a few deep breaths, Mum thanked her and, with her son, cleaned up the mess.

A child dropped a container of milk on the floor and some came spilling out. "Oh dear," said Nana. She put two hand towels on the floor – one for each of them. They skated around the kitchen cleaning up the mess without even using their hands.

When we choose to be responsible for ourselves and all that we may impact, we choose to support the best for every living thing on earth.

acknowledge, by saying out loud, that we have just walked into a chair and hurt our leg, rather than accusing the chair of being in the way. Children will imitate this practice of taking responsibility for themselves and their actions. Rather than defending our right to raise our voice or ignore their request, when we apologise for doing that, children learn to identify and sort out mistakes they make, both physically and emotionally. What more important life lessons can we model for children?

> Taking responsibility for our lives is much easier learned in childhood than adulthood, especially if we've experienced many powerless years of life.

Experience this ...

- **Make a mess, clean it up.** Practice taking responsibility for errors of judgement – physically, socially, emotionally – own up to what you've done in a situation. Choose to take responsibility for your actions, whether intentional or unintentional.

- **State matter-of-factly what children have done.** There need be no judgement; just information about what has happened and consideration, perhaps together, of the possible consequences.

- **Create a song together to lighten those mess-up moments.** Something along the lines of, "When we make a mess we clean it up."

- **All messes need cleaning up, ideally by the person responsible.** Ask yourself, "What do I need to do to make this right?" Model cleaning up messes and say out loud what you are doing, "Oh dear, I've spilt the water; time to clean it up with the tea towel." Or, "I really lost my temper just now. I'm very sorry I shouted at you. That's not okay."

- **Help each other.** Offering to help others clean up their messes also works to support this

message of responsibility: "Would you like some help to sort this out?"

- **Have fun cleaning up.** Create ways together of making the cleaning up of spills, breakages and even relationship messes, fun. This could be singing a song, timing the clean up or counting the sweeps.

- **Practice makes perfect.** Practice together showing care for each other's precious objects. Reduce guidance and involvement with each experience.

- **Leave places and situations in a better state than when you arrived.** What can children do with you to assist? Perhaps sing a wee tune: "How much rubbish can we erase, to leave this place a better place?"

- **Me first.** Model and discuss taking responsibility for your own safety for safety's sake and not simply to avoid being told off. An example is to use your seatbelt, not so you won't be stopped by police but so you will be safer if an accident occurs.

Back to
the earth

Where does our food come from before it hits the supermarket shelves? Where, in fact, is our food originally from in its most basic form? The earth nurtures, sustains and recycles all life with help from the elements such as water and sunlight, along with nature's helpers: birds, bees, and even people.

We can be part of supporting the cycle of life as we enjoy a foray back to nature. We can learn about patience, persistence, and the satisfaction of success while we're at it. How? Well, gardening. This is a time to enjoy the sun on our backs, earth in our fingernails, or the peacefulness of an evening watering the garden patch.

There is enormous gratification in tending our dinner from earth to plate, recognising the nutrient-rich building blocks that have combined to create this expression of life, infused with our love.

Modelling focus and joy in our gardening work will provide superb incentive for our budding gardeners, barely from seed themselves, to get out into the garden. (They may well need to know about how to grow life from the earth as the post-petroleum era draws nigh).

Working together with nature to nourish the growth of flowers, vegetables, herbs and other plants will be a positive expression of your care for each other and for your patch in the world.

Experience this ...

- **Garden plotting.** Together, find a spare plot of earth or fill a pot, basket or trough with earth. Plant a few seeds or transfer a cutting or small plant from somewhere else. Water each evening and enjoy the anticipation of waiting for the magic to be seen.

- **Joy of gardening.** Ask around to find out who enjoys and understands gardening. You may even find you have gardening wisdom at your green-fingertips, passed down through the ages in your own family.

Two friends were sitting outside in the sun, talking and pulling out weeds. A young child joined in without encouragement, perhaps assuming from the adults' actions that, "this is what you do when out in the garden talking."

Respect for life is generated and expressed by nurturing the earth's bounty from seedling through to full growth.

- **A garden of my own.** Offer children a space to have a go at gardening. Provide them with seeds or plants; support them to plan what they wish to grow, help them research how to do that, and get gardening. Talk together about what is going on beneath the surface and, as the shoots emerge, above it. Work together to protect this special garden space.

- **Garden treat.** Here's an extra special treat for children. Display their name in flowers! This is a wonderful opportunity to link children with their natural surroundings. Take the time and effort together to choose a plant, find the seeds, and shape children's initials, names, or even a favourite object, with the seeds. Nurturing your seedlings through to radiant blooms is a wonderful experience and gift.

- **Community gardening.** Consider joining (or creating) a community garden together. Contact your local council which may be able to advise you on how to go about this.

- **Garden adventurers.** Support children as they become more adventurous and wish to experiment more with their garden area.

Set up a regular time to water and weed the garden patch.

Talk everything through with children, empowering them to make decisions regarding choosing the spot, gathering the seeds or plants, planting them and tending them.

Some plants will flourish; others will not and some will wilt and die. Explain that this is just part of the process. Try another plant or seed; move them to another spot for more or less sun; give the seedlings/plants longer or more regular drinks. Give gardening a go. You've nothing to lose.

Appreciate the process rather than the final appearance of the garden or resulting plants. Encourage children to reflect on their gardening experiences by talking about what worked and what didn't and what might be done a little differently next time.

Rejoice when the first shoots appear; when the leaves begin to multiply and when the first bulbs or flowers raise their heads. If you've planted something edible, share the first taste together.

Where do I come from?

The musings of a curious, questioning human being are learning opportunities for both the questioner and the, sometimes alarmed, 'questionee'. How can we answer the it-is-going-to-be-asked-at-some-point question regarding how we came to be, with respect and dignity?

The key is to respond simply and honestly. You don't need to delve into the full details of conception and birth unless specifically asked to. While the facts of your response will reflect your particular family situation, initially, it is enough to offer something like, "Mummy and Daddy made you together. You grew in Mummy's tummy and you were born [at this time on this date]." Later, it could be added that, "you came out through Mummy's vagina," or, "out of Mummy's tummy through a space that the doctors made."

Further details can be addressed as required such as how Mummy's egg and Daddy's sperm got together. This could also involve using picture books about conception and birth, or specifically stating the basic facts about reproduction without embellishment or judgment.

It is useful to have a broad understanding of the varieties of conception and birthing methods we currently have available to us. Much can be discovered by talking with friends and family, or contacting midwives, nurses or other health professionals. Being involved in others' pregnancies or present at births can be an incredibly informative and wonderful experience.

Children can be better than adults at appreciating the wonder and miracle of conception and birth. They are often quite pragmatic about such things, their sense of humour bringing us all back to the human reality of this ancient, natural process.

When supported appropriately, children cope very well with the emotions and intensity of labouring and birth. Witnessing a baby's first breaths and movements is an experience like no other. It is also an immense honour and privilege to be present at such a time. Depending on children's ages and previous experiences, they may be given more details about what is happening. Even the smallest children can be in awe of the fact that a new person is coming into the world.

After being present at the birth of their younger sister, the older two – aged three and five – were playing at 'Midwives and Mummies.' One was leaning over a Swiss ball and making deep groans, while the other reached between the 'Mummy's' legs and helped deliver her baby.

A two year olds' recollection of seeing his little sister having a water birth: "Mummy was crying, crying, crying and Baby came out in the spa."

When we understand and respect how we came to be, we can feel empowered in our right to exist, and in turn support this significant experience for others.

To be open to learning about the beginnings of life and birth, and to be able to share this with children, we may need to consider our own fears or perspectives on a process that we've all been involved in, one way or another. Let's go back to the beginning and again learn about human initiation to this world, while sharing this knowledge and miracle with children.

Experience this ...

- **Tell it like it is.** Give children simple, honest explanations to their questions about how they came to be living human beings. Give increasing detail in response to their age and interest.

- **In the beginning.** Talk with children about their own birth. Discuss how the others who were there felt about that first incredible experience at bringing this brand new human being into our world.

- **Creation expression.** Use role plays, drawings, songs, discussions, and stories to help children understand about life being conceived and birthed. Encourage and appreciate children's input.

- **Baby bonding.** Discuss with children what's happening for someone who is pregnant or labouring, and consider what we can each do to support this new life and the baby's family.

- **How was it?** Talk with friends and family about their birth experiences. How did they feel before, during and after their baby's delivery? What would they have preferred to happen? What would they do differently next time?

- **Get the story straight.** Increase your own awareness of conception and birth options by seeking out people to talk to who have experienced home birth, caesarean section,

Children can be in attendance at both hospital and home births. However, you may have to ask first about hospital regulations and arrange for someone to have your child nearby so as to bring them into the hospital at suitable times.

Avoid pressuring children to, 'be older than they are' and taking on too many responsibilities. Allow them to enjoy the experience and have someone available to support them if they need that.

assisted conception, water birth, medically-aided vaginal birth, doula support, and any other methods you don't yet know about. Raise any concerns or fears and discuss these. Ideally, the person you are talking with can give a balanced view, both of what worked for them and what else is available. They can also offer an insight into the possible benefits and side effects of each. Share what you have learned with children.

- **Consider what society thinks and expects of pregnant and labouring women.** Find out about traditions, expectations, and fears around childbirth. Write, draw or think about your own beliefs to prepare for children asking deeper questions.

- **Experience it.** Support children to be aware of pregnancy experiences and be present at births. Attendance at the birth may not eventuate depending on the progress of the labour but if their presence is not planned for, it is unlikely to occur at all. If you are to be there for the labouring woman, or if you are the labouring woman, then someone else will need to be able to care for and spend time with your child or children.

Many hands make light work ...
eventually

From birth, children can observe and play a part in the household tasks we must do each day. From developing an awareness that the jobs exist to learning simple tasks, children can play their part right through to when they are ready to head off and begin their lives away from home.

The process goes something like this: we do, they watch; we do, they support; they do, we support; they do, we relax (well, maybe not that last one but it's a lovely dream). However it turns out, children need opportunities to increase their skills and participate in the daily management of a household. This is for their own sake, acknowledging the relationships and responsibilities we share when we live together.

One-off jobs – such as asking a child to assist you in cleaning the bathroom – may be how household task contribution begins. After a while, this could become an allocated role for them to play in the household management. Eventually, for the sake of fairness and variety, a roster of tasks could be used to rotate task allocations on a daily, weekly or monthly basis. Even littlies can be involved in all of the tasks we include in the roster: first as observer, then helper, then *oulá!* It's over to them.

Dad asked his eight year old son for some help chopping the veggies for dinner. They chatted while chopping and then the boy said, "Hey Dad, this is really fun doing this with you."

Working together to maintain the home we share empowers our feeling of belonging and builds a real sense of responsibility.

Experience this ...

- **Sing a happy working song.** Do the household tasks with children either observing you or directly participating. For each step, talk about what you are doing, taking notice of whether you're making it sound fun or rather onerous. Perhaps make the steps of the task into a song you can sing together.

- **Cheers for chores.** Acknowledge children's efforts, especially when they act spontaneously to have a go at these tasks on their own. Support their initiative and sense of success by discreetly completing whatever was missed out the first time.

- **Let children do the dishes.** Things to be washed may include recently used dishes or those interesting, hardly-used and dusty utensils at the back of the drawer or cupboard. The children could be happy for many long minutes or even hours. Afterwards, clean up any mess together.

- **Onward and upward.** Create a regular opportunity for children to wash the dishes. Expand the role over time to include clearing away dishes after meals and drying and putting away clean dishes.

- **Cleaning themselves up.** Prepare a space for children to handwash their own clothes. Make an opportunity for children to practice taking responsibility for cleaning up their own messy clothes. Perhaps create a full wash room set up, including clothesline and pegs, for children to really get down to business whenever their clothes get dirty.

- **Think tasks.** Together think about what other household tasks children could participate in and eventually take on as a daily task. Set them up for success and let them have a go at these.

- **Task roster.** Create a roster for household tasks. Perhaps list the jobs to be done on a piece of paper and stick the names of family members beside each. Rotate weekly or as you wish.

The actual amount achieved on each task will differ between children depending on their ability and interest. For example, a baby begins by observing you sorting the washing. Then they may touch and investigate the clean clothes. Later, children can find and take their own clothes from the pile; then, sort other people's clothes and transport each pile to the place they need to go to. Folding can be yet another stage. The more fun and support we provide, the more they'll be keen to persevere and master the tasks.

Always empty buckets after the work is done and never leave filled buckets around.

Be available while children are undertaking these activities. You don't need to hover and could leave them to it and get on with reading that book you've been meaning to for ages. Well, maybe ...

The gift of **touch**

The pleasure and necessity for babies to have regular, loving skin-to-skin experiences with caring human beings is well understood. The same can be said for older children and adults.

Humans are an interdependent species. We need to work together to survive; we need to know others are there for us. Touch offers us a way to directly connect with each other. When lovingly undertaken, touch strengthens the physical and emotional connections between us. Generous offerings of time and attention focus us on the solidity of the relationship and ensure our worth is reaffirmed: "I give to you gladly. You are worthy of my time and energy."

His Mum used to massage him often as a child. Even now, as an adult, a gentle hand on his shoulder or back can energise and calm him.

Children's physical, mental and emotional development can be aided by as little as a few gentle muscle squeezes any day from birth. This combined with a soothing environment and loving words communicates our care for them. Laying a baby on our outstretched bare legs, or sitting beside a child, and gently whispering what we are doing for their body and how much we enjoy their existence is just the tonic for a lasting, secure, and essential attachment relationship.

Beautiful oils, lit candles, soft music or some other tranquil ambience can complete the experience. Children who do not usually enjoy lying still may change their mind when enjoying this special time together. Massage may sooth a crying baby or unsettled child.

When children get a little older they may ask to practice massage on you. Bring on the lavender oil and bare those shoulders – life's about to get a whole lot better.

As the mother of all senses, touch is a truly rewarding gift to both give and receive. When touching others with love we are acknowledging their right to be here, our love and respect for them, and the beauty of this special moment together.

Experience this ...

- **Ooh I like that.** Together consider what feels lovely on your skin and have a go on each other: butterfly kisses with lashes on different body areas; kissing arms; insect walking adventures with your fingers; head massages; foot squeezes; anything is worth a try. However, do stop as soon as you are asked to.

- **Pizza-massages (or other recipes) on each other's back**. First clear the surface. Then you need flour and yeast sprinkled and oil and water drizzled and poured. Now, knead that to a dough before rolling it out. What will be on today's pizza? Sloppy tomato sauce? Chopped capsicum? Scattered herbs? Top with sprinkled cheese and then bake the pizza (sliding palms up towards the head then reversing this once the pizza is cooked). Now slice it up. Yummy! Banana cake next anyone?

- **Offer massages to children of all ages** – from birth to adulthood.

- **Experiment with sensory enhancers in massages:** oils, fabrics, cool metal or stone, rough wood, a swirly shell.

- **Provide a warm, scented foot bath.** Adding lavender or scraped, squeezed lemon works well. Follow with a warm towel-dry and put on socks or slippers.

- **Support children to give you or other people** – even babies – massages. Offer pointers as to what is safe and feels nice for you and discuss how people enjoy different types of massages.

Massaging heads or necks roughly can potentially cause damage so extra special care must be taken. It can be helpful to begin with massaging feet and hands before attempting other body areas.

Always respect the person you are massaging. Ask them if you can massage a certain area and if they do not like it, do not continue.

Baby massage: Choose a calm, rush-free time. You may wish to remove clothes from both you and baby in a warm room so you can have skin to skin time, possibly with a bath ready. Ask baby if they are ready for the massage and wait a moment to detect consent or refusal before you begin. Work out together what they most enjoy.

Where the water
meets the land

Natural, moving bodies of water – whether the pounding of waves on a beach, a creek trickling over stones, or the rushing of a river through the bush – provide us with a sense of wonderment. These often breathtakingly beautiful spots help to create a relaxing, rejuvenating, cleansing or healing experience. They allow space for creativity, perspective, peace, and a sense of bliss. They also offer scope for adventure, exploration, mystery and magic. The possibilities are endless.

At the waterside, we find the very building blocks of life – water and oxygen. The *ancientness* of this vista can remind us of the cycle of nature of which we are a part. It can also offer reminders of our ancestors seeking food on the shores or riverbanks. At the beach, as we smell the ubiquitous salty scent of the sea, we may see shells, their inhabitants long gone, or ground down to sand over millennia. Treasures are to be found at every turn to peer at, to feel, to build with, to wonder about or to collect for a collage or treasure box. Driftwood, stones and shells may be large, small, colourful, shapely, swirly in design, broken, whole, deserted or still inhabited. The sand – how many grains might there be? – may be either squishy or rough beneath our feet. Stones may be challenging for little legs to navigate. The warm sun on our skin or cold biting wind will further enrich our experience. We hear the birds and the waves and, if we listen carefully, even the chatter of the scuttling sand bugs. We might want to taste the gritty sand or lick the salt water or feel the waves lapping up our legs towards rolled up clothes. There may be an enthralling sense of being a little close to danger; the world beyond feeling very close or very far.

There is so much to do and experience near the water's edge – rivers, lakes, waterfalls, little creeks, underground waterways, and emerging springs. Go and explore them.

It was a clear skied day, the first of spring. They drove home via the beach. Someone called out from the back seat, "Let's stop." Hmmm, that wasn't really the plan. There was dinner to cook, there were jobs to do. But she chose to say, "Yes, let's." Pulling over, they hopped out of the car and opened the boot to retrieve the togs and towels that always lived there. Off they went to really experience this first glorious day of spring. Sand, shells, salty air, gentle sun, calm breeze and freezing water – yet they all went swimming. This time together was not forgotten, unlike all those other days of simply coming straight home and getting on with jobs.

Appreciation for the gifts of land and water pass on powerful messages about our right to, and responsibility for, life.

Experience this ...

Be prepared. Take towels (even if swimming isn't intended), sunblock, hats, food, drink, bags for rubbish and containers to collect treasures. Stay water safe.

Respect the fact that living creatures are best left in their own environment, observed and marvelled at from a distance. Ideally, choose a natural wonderland away from human-made distractions such as playgrounds or shops.

Know that there's no such thing as bad weather; only bad clothing. Waterside adventures can take place in all weathers. Remember to take extra care where water can rise quickly during and after storms.

- **Plan a visit to a nearby beach, river or lake.** Allow for spending as much time as you can so that everyone has enough time to explore the area, find treasures and experience the many sensations a waterside adventure can offer.

- **Say yes,** the next time children request a spontaneous visit to any local, natural water source, adjusting your plans to suit. Go when the spirit moves any of you.

- **Express your salty, sandy, rocky or grassy self.** While at the beach or river, utilise as many natural treasures as you can find to create something beautiful.

- **Who's in first?** Experience the water together in whatever ways are safe and enjoyable. Water, land, water, land – hop in and out.

- **Create time for regular return visits.** Book them into your calendar.

Loving
communication

As human beings, we are not meant to act alone in this world. Our whole survival focuses around our collective ability to interact constructively within local and global communities. It is now well appreciated that the ways in which we choose to communicate – both sending and receiving messages through words and body language – impact deeply on our bodies, those around us and even on the wider world. When we react with a message of anger or negative intentions, our bodies generate stress and hostility which radiates out around us. When we choose to respond peacefully, with intentions based on love, the energy we generate also affects ourselves and others.

Children learn how to talk by having their main caregivers talking with them from before birth, modelling give-and-take in conversations. They broaden their understanding of vocabulary, grammar and syntax over time through observation and trial and error. Pro-social communication skills (skills that enable us to work in harmony within our communities and cultures, including verbal, written and body language) are learned as children first utilise their brain's mirror neurons. Children mimic – and later appreciate the context of – what is modelled for them. Later, we begin to negotiate how we communicate together.

There are several key considerations for effective communication. These include: listening and acknowledgement; the intentions sitting behind our communication; the outcomes we are hoping to achieve and supporting emotional expression.

When communications are offered and received with generosity, integrity and openness, there is room for all involved to flourish as human beings. When we shut down communications or interact with blame, shame and humiliation, there is little scope for expansion of hearts or minds. Even a positive judgement, offered prematurely, can cloud the real picture being communicated. We need to come to each new discussion with an open mind and to avoid bringing past experiences to the conversation.

When we acknowledge feelings by stating what they are without judgement, we provide freedom for letting go of those emotions, for not being attached to them, nor being led by them. We can do this both for ourselves and for others.

One day a little boy was telling his Aunty about an idea he had. She was thinking of something else but attempted to "Oh" and "Okay" at the right points. Eventually the boy grabbed his Aunt's face and turned her head to look at him. She finally got the message.

> We communicate to understand and be understood. A world full of understanding, where people feel safe, strong and valued, offers the earth itself a greater chance of prosperity.

By clarifying communication expectations and practicing these daily, we have a greater chance of understanding and enjoying each other, even in times of excitement or traumatic stress. Communicating about communication is an extremely worthwhile pastime.

Experience this ...

- **Early communication learning.** Give a running commentary of what you're doing so as to include children of all ages (including pre-birth) in your daily business. This may involve talking or singing. What decisions can be made outside of your head? What processing of values or consequences can be verbalised? Try using interesting vocabulary.

- **Acknowledge communications.** Listen generously when children are communicating with you. Set aside your own thoughts and feelings in order to fully appreciate their communication. Acknowledge without judgement and clarify their meaning as necessary. Ask, "Is there anything else?" until there's nothing else they wish to communicate.

- **Acknowledge feelings.** Acknowledge your own feelings as existing and as belonging to you. Notice others' feelings with interest but not judgement.

- **Express acknowledgement.** Acknowledge other people's feelings, when expressed, using any form of communication available at the time – at minimum, a nod of the head. Children and adults may need to be offered some words to help them express their feelings positively.

- **Support children.** Acknowledge children's communication attempts for what they are and support initiatives. They will start and you can assist as necessary. What can you offer that will be helpful? Perhaps encouraging nods and "mmm" sounds, suggesting words or offering a hug to help them feel calmer before they continue.

- **Setting expectations.** Agree together how you wish each other to communicate, stating specifically, and without judgement, what outcomes you expect. Agree these together.

The rhythms
of the earth

Humanity is inextricably linked with nature. Our interdependent species is bonded to the earth, reliant on nature's cycles for our survival. Rituals of observation or acknowledgement can help us to understand and feel grateful for the rhythms of our earth. We can take pleasure in what company we have with us throughout these cycles, rejoice in our lives, and in the beauty of the land where we live and the skies above. We can appreciate the life we are all so fortunate to have.

There is perhaps nothing more awe-inspiring than observing a magnificent sunrise. As the earth rotates towards the sun we may feel the majesty of the event and a lift in our spirits as we experience our first conscious breaths of the day. As the fiery ball appears to rise from behind the hills, from beneath the sea or out of the earth itself, it's difficult to resist the contemplation of our own being. At the other end of the day, multiple colours can stretch across the skies as the enormous gas sphere appears to cap the mountains, disappear behind the trees or melt into the paddocks; comforting, calming, refreshing, as we breathe out after the day.

We can also consider the annual seasons. Many people love summertime. Healing sunshine, warmth and fun, longer days to spend together, swimming and rejoicing in nature, perhaps holidays and gardens in full bloom. Then there are others who in summer see the arid fields bereft of water, and the people, animals and plants parched and dying because of drought. Summer cyclones can be amongst the most devastating. Summer brings both life and death, beauty and barrenness, relief and desolation.

Autumn brings tastes of the chills to come though summer may linger through an 'Indian summer'. Autumn harvests are gathered and stored safely before the flooding rains come and wash away loitering crops. Winter can be magical and miserable. Icy frosts, snowy winter wonderlands. A chance to slow down and hibernate, as many animals do, huddling together around a fire, sharing and reconnecting with each other as with Matariki, the Māori new year. Hopefully, we can appreciate the sustenance we have available until the spring crops arrive after their winter sleep. Spring brings new life for plants and animals though sudden frosts may still arrive to claim some of them. We begin to awaken as the days grow longer and the cycle is rejuvenated once more.

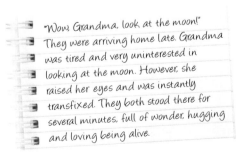

"Wow, Grandma, look at the moon!" They were arriving home late. Grandma was tired and very uninterested in looking at the moon. However, she raised her eyes and was instantly transfixed. They both stood there for several minutes, full of wonder, hugging and loving being alive.

Everything in life dances to a rhythm. Recognition of the rhythms of earth's rotation supports our understanding, appreciation and respect for the bigger picture of life.

If children are not interested in the facts about the sun rising and setting there is nothing wrong with simply witnessing the event together in silence and appreciating the bonding opportunity.

Don't forget to wear eye protection and not to look directly at the sun.

Experience this ...

- **Up to sunrise.** Get up tomorrow morning before the sun rises. If it looks as though it may be spectacular, wake children and view it together from the best spot you can.

- **Setting sun.** View the next visible sunset together. Where is this best viewed from? Enjoy the moment and show reverence for this evidence of the sun and earth working to sustain life in whatever way seems fit for you – silence,

smiles, crazy dancing with pauses to watch solemnly again ... whatever!

- **Seasonal thoughts.** Think about the seasons together. Clarify what you are grateful for; what wishes you have or plans you must make for really experiencing each season where you live.

- **Heavenly rituals.** Create some regular events or rituals to look forward to with the arrival of each season. Consider summer day adventures and nature walks in the evenings; autumn harvests and magnificent sunsets; winter sunrises and cosy evenings snuggled up together or Matariki star gazing; spring cooking and gardening and solstice ceremonies to honour each season. Enjoy these together.

- **Turning, turning.** Discuss the earth's journey around the sun. How our little piece of the world gets closer to or further away from the sun creating our seasons during this journey each year.

A life of **dance**

One of the most connecting times we can have with another person is being held close to them as we dance together, staring lovingly into each other's eyes. Whether by using beautiful music or simply dancing to the rhythm of life, dancing this way can be a memorable event in both children's and adults' lives.

Ask any young child and they'll no doubt agree that there's nothing better than dancing around and playing the fool with adults they love. This is especially true when they're partners in this gorgeous and fun bonding exercise.

Our dance, whether technically precise or wonderfully chaotic, will certainly be great fun for everyone. If going for beauty, old fashioned moves can't be beaten. Dips, sways, twirls, and a reverent bow or curtsey to complete the experience demonstrate far more than just staying in rhythm together. If going for wacky style, forget social conventions and just go for it.

Children love seeing us letting our hair down and allowing them the space to do the same.

Let's delight in our combined freedom of movement, the simplicity of life in the moment, and appreciate the energy-giving and relationship-building side-effects. Go wild! Enjoy.

The spirit suddenly moved her. Her eyes grew dark and mysterious. She reached out her arm, offering her hand palm up. The child took it and gazed up with anticipation. Then they were dancing together, around and around, through her legs, under her arms, stretching wide, leaping high. Their eyes locked then they hugged while their breathing slowed. Off they went back to the tasks they were doing.

Dance brings us closer to other human beings. We can express our innermost selves through dance and in doing so, assist the world in understanding who we are and what being alive is all about.

There are no rules other than respecting each other and working together. Going with it, letting it be whatever it is, is the whole point.

Dance can be done while seated and lying down, too. Dance can be with our eyes, smiles and hearts alone.

Local cultural festivals are a great way to see the vibrant dancing of other cultures. You will be inspired.

Experience this ...

• **Dance, baby, dance.** Play or sing a song that children enjoy or your own made up song. Start dancing or acting it out. You'll know you're on the right track when they stop what they're doing or join in. Let it all flow along with everyone's ideas thrown into the mix.

• **Play 'musical statues' together using a variety of music.** Dance together and when the music stops, freeze in that position.

• **"May I have this dance?"** Invite children to join you or accept their invitations to dance with them. If they are little, hold them in your arms or kneel down at their level. Make it special; make it about them. Share the lead and when you are leading, ensure they feel trust in your lead. Let go! Crazy fun dancing! Anytime! Anywhere! Anyhow!

• **Interpretive dancing.** Describe how you or children are feeling or express interest in a topic or experience through dance. Inspiration can be found from noticing where dancing is happening in the world outside such as the wind swishing the trees, animals moving, birds flying, rain falling. Demonstrate ways feelings can be 'danced.' Have a go together.

• **So many dances.** Many forms of dance abound – which are you interested in? Which do you have access to? Which do children want to join you in? Introduce children to somewhere they can see others dancing: adults or children, exercised based or cultural, planned or spontaneous, it doesn't matter. Join in with the dancing if appropriate. You may feel inspired to create your own performance together.

Death is not the end

We all die. Every single living thing dies. Death is something we will all experience. It is around us, all of the time. We see it and read about it in the media. Sometimes a death occurs in our own family or a friend's family. Our pets may die, flowers are picked and leaves fall from trees. Our ancestors have lived and died before us. Death is under our feet as we trample bugs in the grass and on our skin as we shed old cells to make way for new ones. It is in our food since most of what we eat was once living. Death creates the coral in the sea and the oil in our cars. Death is a natural conclusion to our life and it is the start of new life.

Our bodies will one day decay or be burned, ultimately ending up in the earth and assisting with the growth and nurture of future living things. So continues the circle of life. However, death often presents as an awkward and taboo subject in some societies.

A four year old boy looked at the coffin while at a funeral. He noted loudly, "What a lovely shiny, new box. I wonder what's inside."

"I miss Grandma." "Yes, I miss her too, my darling." "Will I see her again?" "Well, some people believe we will all see each other in heaven after we've died. Others believe that we are all energy and that even those who have died are all around us as part of this energy." "I love you Grandma, thanks for looking after me and I'm glad you can see me growing up."

In my experience, young children handle the idea of death with much more ease than adults. They may furrow their brows and ask whether the person or animal is coming back. They may consider this and state that they will miss the dead being, and they may ask if we – or they too – will die. A respectful answer to this is, "Yes, we all will die one day."

Initially, children tend not to fear death as it is simply another mystery to think about and come to terms with. Religious or cultural beliefs can help or hinder both children and adults in their fear and/or acceptance of death. Concern about what comes after is a persistent quandary for many humans. However, this does not need to develop into a paranoia which will only work to inhibit living a full and satisfying life.

Talking about death with children simply, with honesty and without fear, can be a great gift for them. Acknowledging their reactions and journey is also important. Encouraging a basic trust in nature, in life, in the way of all things, serves to calm and ease any apprehension over this aspect of life. An appreciation of the inevitable death of every living thing as a means of life for others is a healthy way to view death while also offering a way to appreciate new beginnings.

Acknowledging and appreciating death helps us to live fully, in the now. By accepting our own mortality, and that of all living things, we can strengthen our sense of responsibility for honouring every life.

Experience this ...

- **What is death to me?** Firstly, consider your own feelings about death. When children raise this issue – or if the need arises – talk with them pragmatically, and stage-appropriately. Discuss death being a part of all life and that this process will one day involve you and them (hopefully after a long and satisfying life). Offer opportunities to draw or express their feelings in some other ways.

- **Pet farewell.** Hold a funeral ceremony for the death of a family pet or even for other creatures such as insects or birds. This can help enormously with the grief process for you and the children, particularly if the ceremony is conducted from your hearts and with careful thought and planning by all of you together. How can you rejoice in the life that has passed?

- **Visit the graves of those who have died** – whether or not you knew them. Return to honour and commemorate their lives regularly.

- **What are funerals?** Take children to funerals of people you have known. Discuss the different types of funerals you may attend and later reflect with children what they liked and didn't like. There is more freedom in conducting funerals these days; celebration of the dead person's life is becoming more popular.

- **When I die ...** Discuss what you would like at your own funeral with children as soon as they show any interest. They may even come up with some ideas for their own funerals. Promise to honour these requests where appropriate. You may also wish to write down what you discuss.

- **What happens after?** This is a fabulous candidate for using "I wonder ..." statements.

There is no need to linger on any gruesome details in direct relation to a death. This only gives cause for anxiety or, worse, sensationalises our mortality. This can later lead to a numbing of basic human concern for the safety of other living things.

It is sometimes thought that children don't have a place at funerals; that funerals are too serious and overwhelming for children to attend or that the children may get in the way.

However, children need closure, just as adults do. Depriving children of the opportunity to participate in the farewell of someone or something beloved can be experienced as a grave loss for them.

Also, children often have the knack of providing a light-hearted moment to ease the grief being experienced.

Provide children with things to do throughout the ceremony: drawing, knitting, reading, something to eat or drink. They will still be aware of the special nature of this gathering even if they are not paying it full attention.

Rehearsing life

Before books, even before the written word, storytelling has been an age-old form of human expression. Stories have been told since we first walked the earth equipped with a pre-frontal cortex. In many cultures around the world, storytelling is still the main method of passing down information about those who went before, ways that things need to be done, and how 'it' all came to be in the first place.

In storytelling, anything goes. The only boundaries are our creativity coupled with our perceptions about the lives of ourselves and others. Through storytelling, we can practice empathy; what would it be like to be that other person or creature? When we are telling stories, we can play out scenarios that – while they could never happen in real life – we would like to find a way to make them happen. We may be fantasising about how life might be, somewhere, sometime, for someone. Stories can support the modelling of qualities we would like to pass on to children.

After a friend of the family's snapped his Achilles tendon, a little boy created a story of a child who tripped over a log and snapped his Achilles. In the story his friends didn't want to play with him because he couldn't run with them. The story-boy had to endure many sad weeks at home while his Achilles healed. Finally his friends realised how mean they'd been. The story-boy forgave them and they all went running off together. What was he working through with creating this story? The family didn't know exactly but he sure told a great story for them.

Many children love fantasy and role playing: enchanted tales from near and far; goblins and fairies; wizards and wands; magical realms, distant from the boundaries of our world, the 'neverland' that is infinite and unique to each person. To find oneself lost in a charmed forest or in the depths of space is an adventure like no other; it's a totally different matter to being lost in a supermarket. Excitement, anticipation, a new sense of self, and heightened creativity are all wonderful benefits of this type of imaginative play.

Children also love to play out their lives – both real and imagined, from the past, now and on into the future - and transform themselves with whatever they can find as props or accessories to dress-up in. Providing children with time, space and support for their creativity so they can carry out these rehearsals for life is to offer them a true gift. One that says, "I value you and all that you wish to be."

Children are naturally gifted at imagining situations, creating roles, words and worlds. Embracing these – regardless of whether we can see where it's going or understand – is a wonderful way to affirm and encourage the display of creativity. What story shall we tell right now?

Storytelling and playing at transforming ourselves into others provides a training ground for life and an opportunity to practice empathy. We may then choose the best from different scenarios and play them out in our own lives.

Getting involved in children's enchanted tales and super stories needs to be done with respect for what they feel to be important during your time together.

Observe their role plays and ask them whether you can join in and in what capacity. They may say no or they may be quite assertive as to what you must or must not do. All responses deserve respect.

Experience this ...

- **Tell a story you know well** to a child you spend time with. It might be a story about you as a child or perhaps a well-known fairy tale.

- **Sit and watch** (or discreetly listen to if they get stage fright) your child's animated soliloquies. Notice if there are any common themes as this will help you understand their current interests and the ways in which they like to express themselves.

- **Make up a story to tell** and do so with or without props. It can be special to base the story around the children it's being told to, perhaps using their middle names or nicknames. Include their interests and a variety of personalities.

- **Create a story together.** Encourage everyone to have input into the direction of the plot and the grand finale. Support stepping out of comfort zones and stereotypes. This is an opportunity for you all to branch out and really try something new on for size.

- **I'd love to hear your story.** Support children telling their own stories. Give them full attention while they tell their stories and remain respectful to their intentions even if the stories don't make a great deal of sense to you.

- **How might this play out?** Use storytelling to aid yourself and children in working through a particular situation. Try out different scenarios to discover possible outcomes.

- **Search for stories or find books** – local and international – that explain how things are the way they are through myths and legends. Learn these together and tell the stories or act out the myths. Discuss what they tell you and how you feel about them.

Cooking for life and love

I'm inclined to believe English chef Jamie Oliver when he says, "Cook your way to the good life." The creation of culinary delights is one of the most satisfying and joyful of all life's essential activities. It brings us back to earth; back to the basics of what it means to be alive. In many cultures, the making of a meal is revered as a spiritual, meditative and healing activity.

The meal experience is really a series of activities. It begins with growing or gathering the ingredients to planning the meal and savouring the smells, sounds, textures and colours of the various stages of preparation. Finally, satisfyingly, it indulges our senses and feeling of wellbeing as we enjoy the rewards of our efforts.

We can't all be great chefs. However, we can engender a sense of openness and joy when preparing a meal with our children. American author, Barbara Kingsolver, believes that, "Cooking is 80 percent confidence, a skill best acquired starting from when the apron strings wrap around you twice."

Children love to get into the kitchen and create a delicious morsel or three to display, share and scoff.

Choosing a recipe, finding the ingredients, and scooping, measuring, pouring, sifting, chopping, and sprinkling in the correct order also builds children's mathematical thinking processes. Mixing and moulding: well, now, that's straight messy play. This is fantastic for innumerable developmental progressions, including holding a pen, building logical thought patterns, and unleashing the genius artist. Cooking involves many chemical reactions and may need careful timing and observation. Finally, there's the eating – ah, the eating … – to devour the fruits of our own labours is a true delight.

But wait, there's more. Cleaning up can be, oh, so fun as well: sweeping, vacuuming, wiping. Then there are the dishes to be washed: stool, apron, warm soapy water to rummage one's hands around in. Life couldn't get much better really. Go on, find a sturdy chair so they can stand up by the bench – or better, find a low one for them to cook at, string an apron around them, several times if need be, and get cooking. It doesn't matter what!

The girls started experimenting and learning to cook early on with 'free-style cooking.' They knew the basics of what was required for baking and creating many meals. One evening the family took the banana cake the five year old had made, entirely by herself, to Kapa Haka for shared kai. Not one crumb was left over.

Being empowered to provide sustenance for ourselves and others affirms our worth, our value as a human being and strengthens hope for our own future survival.

Recipes with pictures of each stage can be helpful.

Cooking with children often takes longer than when an adult chef is doing the job alone. Embrace this extended period to spend with children but do begin well before meal time. Hungry tummies don't make effective or happy sous-chefs.

Children often choose the same recipe or meal over and over. Perhaps they do not yet feel that they have perfected the process or they just love to eat that one dish. Once they have had enough they will move on. Be patient; repetition is an important aspect of childhood development.

Experience this ...

- **Cooking with children is cool.** Start with easy recipes, perhaps veggie fritters, muffins, basic biscuits or topping a pizza. Choose simple recipes children can really get involved in and which offer rapid gratification. Ignore the mess until later. Children at all stages can contribute from sprinkling, pouring and stirring through to reading the recipes and doing it all. Many will relish the opportunity to practice cracking eggs or chopping veggies.

- **Menu planning.** Have children lead the menu planning and preparation of meals from when they are old enough to have some favourite foods. They can provide the creative initiative and you provide supportive nutritional and culinary consulting services. Children may also wish to lead the way in which the meal is to be presented and eaten.

- **Design picture recipe books** together of children's favourites and their own creations.

- **Cook!** Together, build on your skills to find out how to create a wide range of foods that are most often bought: bread, butter, muesli, yogurt, cheese, soup. Get cooking!

An antidote to **impatience**

The practice of patiently waiting for something is important for everyone. Enjoyment of this experience is also worth striving for. Children are often thought of as impatient. This may be true for children experiencing unmanaged stress while awaiting completion of a task. However, when anticipation is managed and enjoyed, both adults and children can handle waiting and persist with tasks right through to completion.

Anticipation is the experience of allowing ourselves to embrace the truth that 'good things take time.' The experience is enhanced when we appreciate that good things may also require effort and perseverance through the valleys of frustration before we reach our goal.

As adults we may understand – due to our more developed cortex capacities for rational thought – that we cannot have what we want instantaneously. We can choose to distract ourselves while waiting. However, children have a splendid capacity to feel the waiting and the anticipation, focusing their very being on inching towards an occasion or the completion of a task. We can be inspired by children's ability to experience anticipation.

The journey's end is not the only important focus. What we're experiencing along the way also provides opportunities to be all that we can be, preparing us for life.

A young boy understands the joy that anticipation can bring. One of his favourite things to do when having to wait for something exciting is to draw up a grid and write numbers from one to how many days (or hours) he has to wait until the event occurs.

Each time he ticks off a number he beams, perhaps really experiencing the anticipation of this moment. Relishing the knowledge that it is coming.

'Only 67 days until my birthday!'

MON	TUE	WED	THU	FRI	SAT	SUN
PHASES OF THE MOON			1	2	3	4
Full Moon 5 Last Quarter 13 New Moon 21 First Quarter 27				New Year's Day	New Year's Holiday	
5	6	7	8	9	10	11
12	13	14	15	16	17	18
19	20	21	22	23	24	25
26	27	28	29	30	31	

A deep appreciation of life can be derived through skilful management of the pauses and delays inherent in every day.

Experience this ...

• **I'm waiting.** How do you manage the feelings arising when waiting for something to happen? Consider how children around you appear to feel and react to having to wait.

• **Anticipate.** Book in a time to have a special one-on-one occasion with a child. It may be a date, holiday or new experience together. Plan what you're going to do. Affirm the anticipation in one another as the time draws closer by stating how you're feeling as you wait and prepare. Allow yourselves to truly experience the moments with excitement, appreciation, magic and mystery. Notice what is happening in your bodies when you feel the waiting and anticipation.

• **Plan for it.** Prepare for an occasion children are interested in. Consider star gazing where you need to wait for darkness and a clear sky for optimal viewing. Children may like to create a drawn or written tick list to appreciate the anticipation, to keep focused on what needs to happen and to be prepared before the time draws nigh.

• **Expressing feelings.** Create some other ways of expressing anticipation using crafts, dance, stories or other methods and focusing on each waiting moment.

• **Struggling?** When someone is struggling with anticipation, acknowledge the journey so far and wonder what marvels the rest could hold. Model keeping calm while waiting or working towards completion. Perhaps count slowly out loud; keep smiling and take the opportunity to notice your breath. Acknowledge the existence of anticipation with excitement, magic and mystery. Appreciate the opportunity for slowing-down together as you wait or strive for completion of a task or event.

Nature's **treasures**

W're all exploring this world, learning about ourselves, others and life, from the moment we are conceived until the day we die. Those conscious of this path we are all treading make a difference in the world by their intentional and mindful actions; by constantly adjusting and critiquing their understanding of and response to their own experiences and respecting that each action has a direct impact on the world around them.

Babies and children are natural explorers, natural scientists, natural enquirers. Consider this: everything that's now familiar to us was once encountered for the very first time! From the moment a baby's grasp reflex has been brought under control and they can reach out for items to hold, feel, taste, smell, drop and reach for again. They seek a wonderful variety of baby-sized items to discover and experiment with; to help them uncover the answers to "What is the world made of?"

Later, as sensory learning makes way for lessons on consequences and the interaction of objects, sets of different sized and shaped treasure items – shells, stones, seaweed, pinecones, glass, metal, wood, ceramics – can be gathered to support the shifting learning focus to "How does the world work?"

Troves of treasure full of interesting objects delight not only the pint-sized people lying on their backs but older children and adults as well. We can all enjoy the different textures, smells, colours, sounds, tastes and creative potential of the treasures. If the items are mainly natural materials, they can also help create a calming environment for those experiencing them. The vital life force (mauri) of the treasures will benefit all who pause to reflect and delve into the joys of exploring them.

Best of all, it is very inexpensive to create the perfect treasure collection. A trip to the beach, river, bush or your back yard can uncover many wonderful items. Asking friends and family for everyday treasures to contribute – things from nature and all around the house – can add to your treasure trove.

Nature has so much to offer but you have to start looking to be able to find the inherent learning that abounds around us. What can nature offer to teach us today?

While the little baby was touching, sucking and banging his treasure basket items together, figuring out what the world was made of, the older children around him were busy using them for props in their creative play – plates, beds, houses, characters ...

Understanding what the world is made of, and how it works, is essential to us appreciating and caring for our living earth.

Take a bag with you wherever you go, always ready and willing to welcome a new addition to your collection of treasures. Creatures and food items are not appropriate as treasures. Ensure objects for use by infants are longer or broader than their fist to reduce the risk of choking and are not easily breakable.

Do make sure any plant or wood materials included are safe, e.g. don't use tanalised timber and check to make sure sticks and twigs are not from poisonous plants.

A wide based, low rimmed basket is great for providing treasures for a crawling or lying down baby so that they can select their next item without tipping out all the treasures. A bag-full of treasures makes for great storage and easy clear up too.

Experience this ...

- **Basket of treasure.** Create a treasure basket with children using items from around the house, gardens and natural environments. Utilise these in all sorts of play.

- **Collect.** Gather many more items together than you need and give bags or baskets of them away to friends or family, making a fantastic baby shower, birthday or Christmas present.

- **On the look-out.** Whenever you're out and about, keep an eye open for further items to add to your collection.

- **Treasure hunt.** Create a natural treasure hunt with or for children by listing natural treasures to search for outside. Make a list of items to search for: e.g. a yellow leaf, a stone that looks like a ball, a stick longer than your arm … The aim is to find all of the items listed.

- **Thanks.** Show gratefulness for the beauty and perfection of nature just as it is. Make efforts to leave only footprints when appreciating natural settings and take away only what you need.

The life of **our food**

We are what we eat. So, as this is the case, let's consider what our food was before we chose to eat it. How was it conceived, grown, harvested, stored, processed, packaged and transported to wherever we have received or bought it? If we have grown our own, then we know the answers to these questions. For many of us though, finding out where our food comes from takes a little digging as well as some reflection on our values. Part of what we struggle with here is that we may not feel comfortable with the answers we will find.

Meat comes from a living animal that was bred and later killed for the very purpose of feeding human beings. Dairy milk and eggs come from animals as a harnessed side-effect of their reproductive processes. Processed foods often contain chemicals created in a lab to preserve the product for longer, make it tastier, or make the cost of production less by padding out the ingredients. The plant varieties we have regular access to are just some of many that used to be or could be produced; now, only the most cost effective varieties are provided. Foods not available locally have passed through many hands and processes before they end up in our mouths.

Truths about our food need to be acknowledged and appreciated for children to be able to make informed decisions about how they sustain their physical bodies, now and into the future. Engaging in honest conversations about the food we consume and finding out more about its sources can support this.

Some answers are quite insightful, such as the fact that kiwifruit is in season from autumn through to early spring. How fortuitous it is that a high vitamin C fruit becomes available just when many people require immune boosts to ward off colds. Learning about where food comes from can be a challenging and wonder-filled journey to say the least.

At dinner one evening the young children were gnawing on some chicken bones. "Thank you, chickens," Grandad said, "for giving us your meat to make us strong." Wide eyes looked up from the dinner plates. "Thank you, chickens." He said again. "Brk, brk," said one child, turning arms into tucked-in wings and flapping them in delight. "Thank you, yum-yum."

The teacher was blowing an egg for Easter (and a later omelette). A child suddenly crinkled up her nose and said. "But ... that came out of a chicken's bottom!"

A child asked an adult, "How does the chicken decide which eggs to grow a baby chick from and which ones to give us to eat?"

Conscious and effective sustenance of our bodies can occur when we consider honestly the sources of our desired nourishment.

Experience this ...

- **Understand.** Consider your own values and understanding of how our food is produced. Discuss these with children if they bring up the subject or when it seems pertinent. If you don't know the answers, find out together through discussions with friends or family, visiting farms or factories or searching online.

- **Shopping.** When shopping for processed foods, check the back of the packets together. Consider each ingredient and the origins of the item against what is important to you; is it local, natural, ethically produced, etc.

- **Off to market.** Find the nearest farmers' market in your area. Where is it held and when does it open? Go for a visit at different times of the year to discover what wonderful seasonal treasures are there for you to discover in spring, summer, autumn and winter, too. Talk with the growers about what, where, and how they grow their produce.

- **Locavores.** Give it a go finding and using mainly local and seasonal food. Talk with local producers about how the foods were grown. Discuss the food's life-giving elements; nature's gifts to us; the timing of growth and harvesting as well as its fabulous taste, either on its own or in recipes you find or create with children.

- **What about my favourite?** Find out about the journeys your favourite foods have experienced from seed to mouth. How are raisins made? How is bacon produced? How is the oil squeezed out of olives?

- **Get on location.** Find out where your local gardens, farms or orchards are and pay them a visit with children. Pick-your-own fruit or vegetables; buy their eggs, meat or other products. Talk with the owners about how they grow their produce or farm their animals. Consider what it would be like being an animal or a plant here? Discuss with children when they are interested.

Beauty in all

Beauty surrounds us. Some beauty is obvious such as a clear night sky, the sun kissing the shimmering water on a summer's day and a baby's smile. But what about other beauty, not so obvious at first sight?

I remember once walking along the footpath. Spying a small stone, I picked it up and was delighted at my find as I carefully examined it. How smooth it was. What wonderful shades of grey and white. How well it fitted into the palm of my hand, and how comforting it felt as it gently warmed to my body temperature.

By now, the children were looking at me with raised eyebrows and a "Yup, she's lost it" smile. However, I hope they may also have learned something: someone thinks that stone is beautiful. By noticing me revering this seemingly ordinary object, the next time they see something similar, they may recall this little event and find the beauty in another small, seemingly mundane object.

Seeing and catching beauty in both the ordinary and extraordinary has the potential to resonate throughout our lives. Though it be small, plain, and of little consequence to my life, somewhere, someone out there thinks this item – whatever it may be – is beautiful.

It is often said that 'beauty is in the eye of the beholder' and so it can be interesting to discover what others find to be beautiful. In seeking to do this, we may open up to the possibility of beauty in all things and being receptive to seeing how others find beauty in things we may have overlooked.

To see the beauty in something is to recognise a little of its story; its potential purpose in our life and its message. Seeing the best in others and being able to assume their best intentions is helped by an ability to recognise the beauty in the ordinary. People do what they do for a good reason

Coming out one morning to a big argument his children were engaging in, Dad chose to focus on the beauty of getting to see them. "Good morning, good morning, good morning to you. Good morning, good morning, and a happy day to you," he sang while sending them love with both his eyes and his smile. The argument ceased as he hugged one child. Another made toast for them all and the third got everyone water.

Recognising the beauty in everything and being able to generate beauty in the world has positive outcomes for ourselves and life as a whole.

even if their methods are misjudged or their true intention is not clear. This good reason or intention may be found to be beautiful by an open heart.

Those who have known deep happiness in their lives have likely achieved this through recognising and truly appreciating beautiful moments and the beauty in all things. Young children unselfconsciously do this and, in turn, offer us a reminder of the worth of this skill.

By encouraging looking for the positive where only negatives seem to be obvious, we can subvert the more critical eye and the judgements of fear clouding our view of life.

To revere something is to hold it as a real wonder. Stopping to marvel at a natural phenomenon can provide a sense of peace, appreciation and tranquillity. These are qualities we crave in this frenetic world we live in. Whether it be the shape of a branch or the softness of lambswool; the crack and sizzle of a flame; the warm sensation of knowing we are loved; the smell of freshly mown grass or our first lick of a new summer's ice cream, all can be revered as a wonder and considered beautiful.

We can also create beauty. Everything in our day can be articulated with enthusiasm. Consider the warmth of the water while washing our hands; the privilege of climbing into a warm bed on a chilly night or the anticipation of eating freshly made toast while it is prepared. A delight-filled twinkle in the eye can help both adults and children enjoy and appreciate the beauty of any moment.

We can create and express beauty through our everyday attitudes. Being bright, breezy, exuding

vibrancy and enthusiasm and lacing both work and play with magic and mystery helps to blur the lines between enjoyable activities and drudgery. This, in turn, allows children to decide for themselves which activities they wish to engage in and how they choose to perceive these experiences. Opening our eyes wide with excitement, our face brightening with expectation, also does wonders to the way we are feeling and enthrals everyone around us so that they get caught up in what we're proposing, hook, line and sinker.

Experience this ...

- **Beauty stops.** Stop and notice something beautiful about this very moment, either in your immediate surroundings or within yourself.

- **Beautiful me.** What do you find most beautiful about yourself? Body, personality, feelings, actions? Write them down; draw them or tell someone you trust.

- **Beautiful you.** What do you find beautiful about children you spend time with? Tell them. Ask them what they find beautiful in themselves and in you. Help them express it.

- **Beauty all around.** When you're out together, notice the beauty in your surroundings. Stop and describe what you find beautiful. Enjoy it. Perhaps the beauty of a rose in full bloom on the way to the shops; the impressive lines of a vintage car parked nearby or the shimmer of the sun on water.

- **Beautiful journey of life.** What beauty can you see in what's currently going on for each of you in life? Pause to appreciate whatever beauty you find.

- **Keep it forever.** Gather together some of these memories of beauty over time in posters or poems.

- **Dig a little deeper.** What else could you appreciate about you? Look deeper at who and what you are without comparing yourself with others.

- **Assume the best intentions in yourself and other people.** Impart the beauty in what you see in them and what they are intending. Greet a mess – your own or a child's – with, "How exciting, another learning opportunity for us."

- **Nature's beauty.** Consider what is beautiful about a natural item. The smoothness of that plain old stone or the multi-colours in a bedraggled leaf. What potential has it? What preciousness? What attractive characteristics? What has it experienced during its life?

- **Silver lining.** There is always beauty. Find it in a difficult situation and describe it for all involved. What opportunities does it provide? Where is the silver lining? How can you express it?

- **Magic in the moment.** Look for the thrill available in everything. Even impatience can be converted to anticipation with a little creativity and sparkle. Consider all sensory experiences, emotions and interactions.

- **The gift of a smile.** The easiest way to add beauty to you? Smile! The easiest way to add beauty to situations? Smile! The easiest way to add beauty to others? You guessed it ... SMILE!

- **Mutual admiration society.** Gaze into each other's eyes, delighting in being together and in being alive.

- **Beauteous display.** Gather beautiful items with reverence and display them for your own and others' benefit.

- **Beautiful interactions.** Greet the next person you meet or bump into with a welcoming acknowledgement, enthusiasm, vibrancy, maybe even a sparkle in the eye.

- **Magic making.** Consider what reverence and beauty you can bring to each task, each communication, each situation and commit to creating that beauty.

If children wish to describe the beauty they are experiencing and cannot, they may need us to offer them words to do that. This is a wonderful opportunity to acknowledge that it is a special moment when you find or create beauty in life.

Taking time for reverence of life can take exactly that: time. In our overflowing daily busy-ness, it may also take dedication and prioritisation to allow enough time for practicing reverence and acknowledgement of beauty. Choose times free of obligations to begin initial experiments.

Anything can be beautiful: flowers, candles, smiles, genuine relationships, listening to each other, respect, love, awareness, colours, materials, shapes, tastes, sounds, smells, vibrations, difficult situations …

Beauty can be expressed with words, with a pause, with a drawing, a song, a dance, a movement, a quiet smile, a simple turn of the head …

All creatures
great and small

Animals, whether they are wild or pets, provide special opportunities for children to practice making a difference in the world.

People of all ages enjoy watching birds, spotting them amongst the branches and listening hard to hear their tuneful calls. Their songs bring the bush to life; many magical melodies harmonising amongst the trees. We can appreciate the soothing, powerful life force rejuvenating our spirits as we crunch or slop through green wonderlands searching for "the one with the dark feathers and white cotton thing on its neck that sounds like a flute," or spying a fantail trailing our footsteps as we disturb its prey.

Insects and spiders abound in and around most homes. These creatures are living beings just as we are. They have the same rights to this piece of the earth we all co-inhabit. They are going about their daily business, oblivious to our perhaps perplexed concerns about their six or eight-legged appearance. Death occurs daily in this planet's life cycle but it does not have to happen as a conscious act at our hands without necessity. Perhaps the creature is stuck inside our house and would be really rather grateful to be let outside. Perhaps you'll feel better if they continued their life outside your house. If this is necessary, it can be done gently, with empathy and respect.

Fish are fun to watch as they glide or dart through the water. What colours are they? What shapes? Where may they be heading? Do they remember you from their last pass around?

Household pets can be an effective way to learn about other living animals and how they may need to be cared for. Feeding the neighbour's cat while they're away or taking their dog out for a walk can be an enriching experience for children. Where do they like to be patted? What games do they like to play? What is their favourite food?

From here we can discover more exotic animals we may find on farms, in zoos and in the wild. Visits to farms can provide an opportunity for bravery. It really takes something to walk up to a cow and have it lick your hand with their raspy, strong tongue! Zoos have experts who can answer questions children may be intrigued about. Then there are those creatures in the wild …

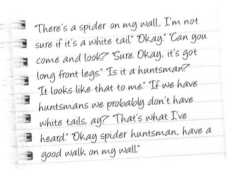

There's a spider on my wall. I'm not sure if it's a white tail." "Okay." "Can you come and look?" "Sure. Okay, it's got long front legs." "Is it a huntsman?" "It looks like that to me." "If we have huntsmans we probably don't have white tails, ay?" "That's what I've heard." "Okay spider huntsman, have a good walk on my wall."

All life is precious. When we treat living things we encounter with respect, our own precious life develops greater meaning and the bonds connecting us to others are strengthened.

Experience this ...

• **Creatures great and small.** Notice any creatures in or around your house. Spend time together watching them go about their daily business. What are they doing? What is life like for them? What rights do they have to a good quality of life? What can you do to make their day easier?

• **Visit your local pet shop.** Discuss what care the pets need and, where appropriate, interact with them respectfully. Empathise with what their life may be like in the pet store and how they might feel being taken to a person's house as a much wanted pet.

• **Pet care.** Help care for your own or neighbours' pets together.

• **Getting close.** Visit a farm or petting zoo and consciously interact with and care for the animals respectfully, delighting in the moment.

What can each of you gain from this adventure together? Go bush. Visit your nearest bush area together and find as many creatures as you can. Talk quietly about their size, shape, colouring, movement patterns, where they are, what they may be doing and what they sound like. Talk about what animal life you might not be able to see e.g. nocturnal animals or micro-organisms.

• **Pet play.** Play together at being various creatures. Have children take the lead to run the game.

• **Creature learning.** Learn about a variety of birds, insects and other animals as your children's interests lead you. Discuss where they live, whether you could visit them, any issues they are having in the world such as predation or being close to extinction for other reasons. What could you do to help with their protection?

Let's be
children again

Freedom from cares is possibly the greatest drawcard adults see children as having. Wouldn't it be great to lose ourselves in the present, without caring about the judgements of others; without worry for the future; to just live in the moment? Imagine being truly free? Of course, it's prudent to abide by society's laws – more or less – though we adults seem to cite society's customs as our reason for holding back from tasting this freedom. Perhaps, this is sometimes an excuse.

Consider this. It's a sweltering hot day. There is a paddling pool with water in it. What may go through an adult's mind: "I feel hot. I wish I could cool down in that water. I couldn't possibly climb into that pool though. What would everybody think? I don't have a bathing suit. I don't want my clothes to crease. Maybe it's not so hot after all. I'd better stand out of the water's reach so I don't get wet. I'll keep my eye on the children though. Look, they're having fun. It really is hot isn't it?" What may go through children's minds, "I feel hot. There's some water. I'm going in!"

Children have their own agendas though they are very often working, in the moment, with the emotional, exploratory and instinctive parts of

their developing brains in the lead. We do not know most of the time what their reasons are for doing something or where their intentions lie. We can only observe children carefully to give us clues as to their thoughts and feelings. We can also try tapping into our own 'in the moment' brain processes. Playing with – or without – children is a great way to relearn how to be free like a child.

What might that play be? To dance and sing for joy. To stop and experience an exquisite moment for a trifle longer than is usually considered appropriate. To float around in that large paddling pool on that sweltering day and not care for anything but the swirl of the cool water around our body. To love the moment. To experience the childhood joy of living in the moment.

A young-at-heart woman enjoyed spontaneously letting loose and running around wildly while singing or making strange noises. It felt great for her and never failed to elicit grins from her children. Although sometimes their friends gave a look of, "What is going on?"

Be free to play, free to love life, free to live in the moment.
Everyone will benefit.

Experience this ...

- **Observe children going about their business without interrupting them.** Imagine what they may be thinking, feeling and doing. Perhaps tiny bits of paper laid out all around the table are to do with maths, or making enough of something for everyone, or thinking of stars, or maybe something else. Notice what elements of their play appeal to you.

- **Recall for yourself what life may have felt like as a young child:** attempting new things; going through different phases; having various relationships and doing things that you liked and enjoyed doing. You may be inspired to try something completely new.

- **What can you learn from children?** Practice being a child. Try swimming in shallow water; creeping about and hiding. Let go of rigid body control and see what happens. Re-learn how to play. Have a go at playing 'silly buggers'.

- **Go with the child in you.** When are you tempted to do something a little wicked; a tad delicious? Consciously decide to give it a go. Choose to say "yes" to yourself. Afterwards you may wish to tell children what you wanted to do and what your experience was like. They may well be very impressed with you; or perhaps not, as they live this way every day.

- **Just do it!** Commit to doing one crazy, instinctive, wonder-filled expression each day. Delight in the joy of being you and life itself. Be free!

- **Switch roles.** Play together with you as the child and they the parent. What will they come out with? How will they treat you? What will you end up experiencing together?

Food **glorious** food

We need food for life: it's essential for vitality, growth and development. Truly appreciating the phrase, "We are what we eat," is the key to understanding the critical importance nutrition plays in our overall wellbeing. Everything we take into our body has the potential to become a part of our body. Every cell needs energy and nutrient building blocks. It is helpful to discover what nutrients our bodies use for various growth and healing functions.

Our enjoyment of food is often rooted in our earliest experiences. Regular, pleasurable, familiar dining occasions can have a lasting and positive impact on our attitude to food and its consumption.

Talking enthusiastically about all foods – both known and those yet to be tried – is helpful. Introducing new foods can be an art. Perhaps create a lively discussion around the possibility that our taste buds may very well adore this new sensation and our tummies will appreciate this boost to growing our bodies. Positivity is key to encouraging children to try new foods. Gently introducing foods and creatively presenting them may help with their

introduction. Children can't help but be impressed, at least with your efforts. Our aim is to assist children in appreciating the joy that food can be.

What's the next meal going to look, taste and feel like?

Experience this ...

- **Beautiful presentation.** Have a play at how you display foods. Shape rice or potato using a little water. Dinosaurs or insects can be created with a little thought. Toast and veggies can be chopped in to geometric shapes. Don't forget that children, too, make great designers. Display all food thoughtfully to show respect and care for both the food and the person you are serving.

- **What's in the order?** Most foods seem fairly appealing when our tummies are hungry. Provide a plate of vegetables perhaps in a rainbow for children before the remainder of the meal arrives.

"What's this?" he was asked while cooking dinner and sprinkling in some spices. "Would you like a taste?" he offered. Soon he had a little plate with a variety of herbs and spices ready for tasting and a large glass of water beside it in case of encounters with unpleasant flavours. What an experience for a child!

Appreciating food and eating supports our physical health and overall wellbeing, helping us be the best person we can be for ourselves, for others and for the world.

- **Munch, crunch.** How many times can you chew each mouthful?

- **Try raw foods.** Many foods are better for us if they are raw. Experiment with a plate full of raw food, laid out beautifully, for you to snack on with children.

- **Empowering healthy eaters.** Have healthy snacks available at any time for children to access on their own. These might be fruit in a bowl on the bench, chopped carrots, roasted vegies or boiled eggs ready in the fridge. Whole foods are best unprocessed and unwrapped. Children could prepare their own snack plates.

- **The whole point.** Next time you're eating satisfying, healthy foods, talk with children about what the goodness is doing for your bodies and how bodies need a healthy diet to keep strong and functioning effectively. Answer children's questions about diet with lots of positives about healthy foods.

- **Can I do it?** Make it possible for each person to serve their own food, and other people's when appropriate. At other times children can be served by an adult or meals could be served before reaching the table and placed in front of them, as if in a restaurant.

- **Eating is a sensory experience.** Providing a variety of different foods to discover together through all your senses can be quite an adventure. Offer somewhere for children to spit out food they don't like; they'll be more open to giving new tastes a try.

- **Crazy bonding.** Many foods make very satisfying munching sounds. Put your ear to the other's cheek and listen close while they crunch for a little light bonding over snacks.

Even if your work of art is turned down, take pride in your creation and vow to repeat the masterpiece again with even greater pizzazz on the next occasion. Be aware that sometimes children need to be presented with a new food on multiple and I'm talking seriously multiple occasions before they will try it. Perhaps their taste buds are not yet ready to accept the new flavours. Keep 'Green eggs and ham' in mind, though don't push them onto a train or into the rain to try it!

Insisting children eat everything on their plate deprives them of their right to learn to trust their own bodies and acknowledge when they are full. When we already feel full, we are even less likely to enjoy foods we are forced to eat.

Food and play don't go together. Firstly, it is not respectful and can be wasteful. Secondly, playing with food can be unhealthy for us if we are to eat it later.

The gift of **age**

We all have something to offer in each stage of our lives: as babies, children, teenagers, adults and as older adults. Older adults in your life may be grandparents or great grandparents, great aunts and uncles, neighbours, long-time family friends, or those you meet in the street or at the park. Some elderly people may live with their extended family, alone or in retirement villages.

Some may be feeling fit as a fiddle while others may be struggling with daily life due to illness and loss of mobility. They may be squeezing as much as they can out of this end of their lives or be confused about how to best contribute in this modern world. Many remember their childhoods well and – having led interesting lives – are keen to tell their stories and share their wisdom. They may be surrounded by friends or family, or spend much of their time alone. They may be the visitor or the visitee, the parachuter, the bike rider or the walker. They may wish they were able to do these things. All have something in common: they all have experiences to share and stories to tell.

Elderly people deserve care and respect. They can offer a wonderful gift of insight into previous generations through their memories and lived experiences. Having seen many changes in the world throughout their lives, they will have stories, learning and wisdom worthy of our attention. They have lived before the dependence on modern technology. They are people who have cared for others, loved others, experienced joy and grief and continue to do so.

Children are often intrigued by the different appearance elderly people have from younger generations. Children may enjoy the different sounds of their voices and the unabashed, cheeky way some older people may interact. Perhaps children serve as a reminder of the natural course of things – the old making way for the young – or to lighten a sombre mood. Perhaps children encourage the previously dormant child-spirit to emerge again from the young at heart.

The elderly were cared for during their childhood and now, in the winter of their life, may be once again in need of care. Children offer a special ingredient to elderly relatives and friends at this stage of their life: the joy and gift that is childhood.

A young boy was intrigued by what it meant to be 'old'. During a supermarket shop he spoke with two people an older woman with grey hair and a slightly younger woman who had lots of laugh lines. "Are you old?" he asked each of them. The younger woman wasn't so enamoured of being called old, so his Mum said, "He's enjoying finding out about different people's ages." At this the younger woman smiled kindly at both of them and continued on. However, the older woman beamed at this delightful little boy who'd noticed her and said, "Yes, I am, and you're young aren't you?"

Children learn care by being cared for and caring for others. Care and interactions with those whose lives are rich with stories, knowledge and insight enriches our own and others' experience of life.

Experience this ...

- **Ring-ring.** How often do you have contact with elderly people in your usual week? Consider this and what form that contact takes?

- **Talk about age.** Together with children, discuss the older people you know. Who are they? What have their lives been like? What wisdom have they shared or you suspect they have? What needs may they currently have? If you don't know the answers to these questions, ask them.

- **Smile.** Smile and acknowledge elderly people with a positive attitude – friends or strangers – when you next meet them.

- **Knock-knock.** Visit older adults together, both those who you know and those you do not know well, such as someone who lives down your street or people in a retirement home. Ask them questions about their lives. Perhaps turn these visits into regular occurrences.

- **Kindness.** Do something kind and fun for those you have met such as putting on a short concert, making cards, giving them baking or homemade gifts.

The world in **song**

There's a song for everything. There's a song for everything.
There's a song, there's a song, a song for everything.
(Sung to a repetitive, simple tune.)

When was the last time you burst into song? Children love to sing: alone, with others, spontaneously. Whatever, whenever. They love it even more when adults sing with them. It doesn't matter how well we think we can sing. It's the singing that counts. We don't need to worry about what others think about our singing. We can simply enjoy the exhilarating experience of vocal expression.

Songs can be made up on the spot or passed down through generations. We can add our own little flourishes or stick to what we have been taught. Singing is something we can do on our own, with someone else, or with lots of other people. We need no reason to sing and, best of all, anything can be sung about.

Singing is relaxing, inducing the brain to release endorphins and oxytocin, the hormones that create a sense of calmness, happiness, bonding and wellbeing. It is also a great way to express what's going on in our lives or how we're feeling. Songs can be fun and carry little meaning or be deeply potent with self-expression. Songs can help us and others make sense of our lives and world.

Due to the feel-good hormones released when singing or listening to others sing, our human brains learn very effectively when lessons are sung to us and by us. The lessons carry more relevance and meaning for us as the presence of endorphins not only has us want to continue this activity, it goes on to stimulate the release of dopamine, further aiding our motivation to take notice and act on what's being asked of us. Singing together while out walking or during long journeys can help us remember these enjoyable experiences together for many years.

We need no equipment to sing. Our own voice, however it sounds, is all that is required. Every person can participate, even if only smiling while humming snippets of the song.

Our voice is a precious way to express feelings about life and share these with people we love. Just start singing!

One day she sang a little ditty to her four year old girl, along with a big smile, "Dar-ling, come and get your shoes on." She responded with a lovely sing-song voice following Mum's tune, "Mum-my, no no-no no-no no."

> Singing lightens moods, nourishing our bodies with positive hormones, helping us to love and learn together.

Experience this ...

- **Sing what you're saying.** Whatever you wish to say can be sung. Try using a sing-song voice with your next words, whatever they are. Create a mini musical with your everyday interactions together.

- **What else to sing?** Talk together about what songs you know or have heard and write them all down.

- **Get singing.** Sing songs on your own or together whenever you feel like it. Sing in the car, walking to school, while doing jobs or in the bath. What do you love singing together at the moment?

- **Learn more ...** Listen out for new songs and learn as many as you can. Be open to a variety of languages, styles and topics. Look for songs on specific topics to support children and what they're currently learning about (say, climbing or gardening), interested in (perhaps rainbows, cars, water) or needing at this stage of their life's journey.

- **The world in song.** See if you can sing a song for any occasion or topic that comes up.

- **Create your own simple songs about what you're doing in daily life.** Use a standard tune and formula so that children get the gist of what you're doing and can use their own words. These songs can help to make jobs fun and maintain focus.

- **Sing your love.** Devise special songs for children in your life; songs about them and the beauty of your relationship with them.

- **Create songs without words.** Instead, make interesting sounds together to fun beats.

> We learn songs most effectively by hearing them over and over again and joining in when we feel ready. It can be helpful to have the words written down although most children learn more quickly than adults without needing to see the lyrics. Now, there's a challenge!

Working it out **together**

There had been an ongoing problem with the youngest child going into her older sisters' bedroom without asking, playing with their things and sometimes taking those she wanted to. The older girls were upset about this and asked that everyone agree some rules. They wrote out an agreement, Kendra needs to knock before going into Lucy and Sophie's bedroom. If no-one is in there, she musn't go in. Only if the answer is, "Yes," can she go in. Everyone agreed to this. Then Kendra had fire in her eyes. Off the couch she leapt and found a piece of paper and pencil. With a determined and aggrieved voice she spoke out loud the words that her scrawls on the paper meant, "People must knock before going into Kendra's room. They can only go in if Kendra says, "Yes!" Fair call, Kendra. Together, they adjusted the 'rules agreement' to state in general that people needed to knock before going into anyone else's bedroom.

Negotiation is a key communication tool. It can be easily practised and modelled with children as the need for resolution of issues arises often. Negotiation consists of noticing there are differing perspectives, listening to all relevant points of view, questioning, clarifying, and then resolving the differences by making a decision together.

Many times each day we may find that our opinions of what needs to happen next differ to those of the children we are spending time with. Children, like adults, appreciate being consulted regarding decisions affecting them. Empowering children to engage in negotiation processes will help them learn many skills while also feeling valued and knowing that they have some control over what happens in their lives.

It's good to question and be questioned. We can deepen our understanding or make a shift in our thinking when we participate in discussions and conversations and when we enquire with curiosity and openness to change. Examining a situation or perspective allows clarification. It also provides an opportunity to hear another's view point or an interpretation we may not have considered or even thought about.

When we work together to arrive at a solution, we are all affirmed for our contributions, in turn fuelling our desire to further contribute to the world.

Engaging in a robust round of clarifying feelings, reasoning and checking facts where needed, does more than simply affirm an already good decision or improve on a situation found wanting. It provides ample opportunity for building communication and cooperation skills as we work together to find the best resolution for everyone involved to move forward.

When we negotiate we have an opportunity to practice communicating with respect, patience, curiosity, and persistence. We may find out we did not have all of the information, or that our logic was flawed. We may discover there is more than one right outcome or perspective. Armed with a better understanding and once all is successfully settled after discussion, we can move forward with confidence in the decision that we have reached together.

When negotiating, it is helpful to listen more and talk less, while ensuring that no one is left feeling hurt or unheard in the process. This can be achieved with all parties being both respectful and compassionate to each other during the discussion. All participants need to feel they have been treated as equals during these communication experiences.

Sometimes the negotiation needs to stop until all parties are ready to re-engage. Many people need time and space, free from pressure, to process information and recognise where they are at before they can participate in decision-making.

Bringing real life reasoning to the negotiation assists with children's buy-in which, in turn, leads to happier willingness to engage with the decision-making process and eventual outcome. "Because I said so" is not a real life reason. "Because I really need your help right now. Otherwise we won't have time for the game we were planning" is.

There are times when negotiation is not possible or useful in the moment. Reflect on these situations together at a later opportunity.

Negotiation cannot occur when one or more is feeling stressed or unsafe. We need to support the calming down of both ourselves and children before logic, reasoning and communication can be utilised effectively.

Experience this ...

- **Starting negotiations.** Consider how you usually negotiate. Do you initiate negotiations or engage in them only when you must? How do you feel during the process and after negotiations are complete? Are you open to things that have already been agreed being re-negotiated?

- **Let's talk about this.** Agree together about how to initiate negotiations such as asking, "Can we talk about this?" Once agreed, ensure this initiation is treated with respect and attention. There is clearly one party unhappy with the current situation. If you can stop and negotiate now it is usually worth it. However, it may be that discussion must happen later. For example, when you all need to leave the house now as you have an important appointment, this is non-negotiable. However, you could agree to talk about other options for next time while you're travelling to this appointment.

- **We're in this together.** When negotiating, give real and fair consideration to each other's points of view, information and suggestions. Model respectful listening and open communication and give up the need to be right.

- **Solution maker.** "Hmmm, I wonder ...," or, "What do you think?" are splendid responses to open the way for children to consider solutions themselves and balance their contribution in the negotiation process. For example: "But why do I have to come with you to pick up Lucy from school?" "Hmmm, what do you think?" pausing patiently. "Because I'd be alone in the house and might hurt myself?"

- **Deal maker.** You can make a deal showing you both agree with the outcome or decision after a negotiation session. I touch knuckles with my children and we look each other in the eye as we say, "Deal." It's also useful to agree on consequences should the deal be broken.

- **Choice.** Try using choices as an element of the negotiation process with the choices you offer being suitable to you: "We need to go home now. Would you like to run, walk or skip home?" Or you could agree information and boundaries and the children take it from there. "It's dinner time. We need to use up some food in the fridge tonight. What would you like to eat?"

- **Real life reasons.** Carefully work out what the real life reasoning is for your point of view by considering why you believe they or the situation must work in this way and how it assists the world. For example, "You must go to bed now so that you will have enough energy to enjoy our special day tomorrow," as opposed to "Santa won't bring you any Christmas presents."

- **Open Sesame.** Practice being open to re-negotiation. It's okay for people to change their mind and request a rethink. Perhaps life's cause and effect process has taught them a lesson since the initial negotiation or they just feel differently right now.

- **Supportive environment.** Support negotiation between children as necessary. Ideally adults will stay out of the process as long as possible to enable the children to have a good go at working the issue through themselves. When assisting, it's helpful to begin by stating what you have noticed and summing up the situation before handing over to the children again. Then, observe again. If more input is needed, make suggestions for next steps but still leave it in the children's hands.

- **Making hard work fun.** Come up with fun ways of setting the negotiation scene together. Perhaps you roll or throw a ball to each other while negotiating or the person who is speaking holds it. You might find lying down outside is a most conducive negotiation environment. Get creative together.

Never too early
to be prepared

Preparing for a Civil Defence or other emergency can be off-putting for many of us. The fear of what might happen paralyses some into inaction. For others, this task seems too difficult; too much work, or simply something that keeps falling off the 'to do list'. However, if an emergency was to occur, all the effort that went into preparation would be well worth it.

Children love to assist with projects and can do a splendid job of keeping the fun in tasks. Putting together a Civil Defence kit and practicing emergency responses provide excellent learning opportunities for children. What will we need to do, eat, see with and find out? How much water might we need? How would we open these cans? What will our pets do? Where could we all meet up? How do we raise the alarm in an emergency?

Discussing possible emergency events and the situations that could create a Civil Defence emergency equips children with skills to assist themselves and other people. For some emergencies, they may need to stay in a certain place until someone comes to find them. For others, they may need to meet at a pre-arranged rendezvous.

Action helps us move through fear. How could I best help myself and others to survive if a disaster or emergency should happen? Consider this question for yourself and support children to begin doing so as well. Get prepared!

> When the children were asked, "What shall we talk about tonight?" Around the dinner table, the youngest would often say, "Let's talk about disasters." He had his family preparing for all kinds of potential troubles. Due to his interest, they all knew where the main water tap was and where to meet if they had a fire.

When we are open to discussing life's possible disasters with children, and working together to prepare, we are empowering them to take responsibility for their own lives and the lives of others.

Experience this ...

• **Talk about it.** Discuss the different types of disasters which create emergency situations such as earthquakes, volcanic eruptions, fires, tsunami, power cuts; or a medical emergency when an ambulance is needed.

• **Planning.** Plan what actions may be needed in each of these situations. Plan how to get help and communicate with each other to ensure you're able to be safely together again. Perhaps you're in different rooms of the house or some of you are not home. What about your neighbours or other family members? What do you need to do if you are away from home during an emergency? Everyone will have something to contribute.

• **Practice.** Practice and review your plans together regularly – perhaps every two or three months – or whenever children bring up the subject.

• **Know the way out.** When out and about, discuss emergency exits. Look for standard emergency exit signs and practice weighing up the options where they are not obvious. Practice.

• **Emergency list.** Put a list of emergency phone numbers in a sealed plastic bag in children's bags so that they can get help to contact appointed adults if they need to.

• **Get kitted out.** What would you need in a Civil Defence kit? Put together a list of items. Gather these as you go about your usual household or shopping routines. Together, pack all the items into a Civil Defence box or bag. Where should the kit be stored?

• **Kit review.** Allow children to go through this kit as they wish – or at least every six months – and take the opportunity to replace soon-to-expire food, water and batteries to ensure that all items will be ready when needed.

Keep descriptions as simple and factual as possible. Avoid sensationalising the possible impact of emergencies and disasters and their fallout.

Reassure a fearful child with calm, pragmatic discussions about your action plans and the very low chances of such events occurring. It is not a bad thing to talk honestly with children about life being a risky business.

Plans can be displayed in many ways. Children are super creative when given the opportunity. What can they come up with?

City Councils, libraries, the Civil Defence website (www.civildefence.govt.nz), and phone directories are good places to start looking for support information.

Repair it. **Reuse it.** Recycle it.

Everything we have is a privilege. We are privileged to be able to get it and we are privileged we are able to keep it. Being mindful of what we have materially, enables us to come to a full understanding of this privilege, especially when so many have so little.

But what happens to the product or item – and its packaging – when we no longer wish to own it; or it has served our purpose? Where does it usually go? Perhaps into our rubbish bin. And where next: to the landfill. And once there, what happens to it? It sits, and sits, and sits. If the world is lucky, it may decompose within a few long months or years. Disturbingly, some materials will not break down during either our lifetime or that of the next generation. By then there will be more mountains of such waste sitting, and sitting, and gradually – or maybe not at all – returning to the earth.

Mass consumerism and the disposal of its wasteful by-products is everyone's problem. We all have the responsibility to maintain this planet. If we don't our children and our children's children will be paying the very hefty cost for our actions (or inaction!). Our waste-full-ness today will impact directly on the quality of life of our future generations.

Something can be done. Repairing, reusing and recycling are some ways to reduce the amount of waste build up for which we are directly responsible. Our children will appreciate having the

The scraps go to 'the chickens' that live just down the road. Sometimes the children are given some eggs to bring home. This is recycling at its most immediate and obvious.

skills to identify repairable, reusable and recyclable items. This will empower them to be able to control wastefulness in their own lives as they help to look after their planet.

Carefully monitoring our own attitude to common 'throw away' tendencies is an interesting place to begin. Have we succumbed to the seemingly harmless habit of tossing everything in the bin, hidden away until – once a week – it is picked up to be disposed of and forever forgotten?

Repairing and reusing

Children take in all that we do. When they see us consciously considering what we do with things that are no longer working properly or not wanted, they have a chance to understand recycling. They see the benefits of replacing their buttons; glueing toys back together, or carrying their togs in a reuseable plastic bag. All children can be nurtured from birth to appreciate what is still useful or salvageable amongst the things they may be tempted to throw away and to act ethically.

Let's support children in working out how to repair and reutilise stuff early! Imagine how much more care children would take of their possessions once they've been involved in the fixing of things they have broken. Consider the creative learning opportunities of finding ways to use an apparently useless item. There are wonderful potential side-effects of having children see repair or reuse as 'first stop' options before throwing something out and buying something new.

Recycling

Many New Zealand city councils make it easy to have recycling taken from the kerbside along with rubbish collection. Children may happily take on the recycling responsibility once they

Our choices of rubbish management will impact directly on the health of the land and the living, both now and for the future. Our children's children will have to work with the earth in whatever state it is left for them.

understand where the things in the bin go to and the consequences of over-filled landfills on future generations. This understanding gives them the realisation that they can make a difference. Also, remember the original recycling method: composting. Stinky, yes. Flies, yes. Great for the garden, YES! Compost systems are nature's ingenious way of recycling the food we are lucky enough to have left over, breaking it down to nourish the growth of future plants.

Worm farms are another way to efficiently breakdown organic matter into splendid fertiliser. It's fascinating to observe this process in action. Another option for recycling our leftovers is to feed them to animals. Consider setting aside food for a neighbour's chickens or feeding bread to a local duck population.

We all benefit when we provide opportunities for children to satisfy their curiosities. By consciously managing our rubbish, we can support children to work out the missing links about the journey of all things and the cycle of life. We are all part of that cycle, both in life and in death.

Experience this ...

- **Refuse review.** Take a peek at your habits of getting rid of rubbish and dealing with broken items. Consider where you sit on a continuum of 'repair, reuse or recycle' through to 'dispose of it' for different types of items. What's being modelled?

- **Repairing, reusing, recycling.** Discuss with children what alternatives to 'throwing it out' are available at home and in your community. Include these starters:
  - where could shoes, clothes or books be taken to be repaired? Could you mend them yourselves?

Just about everything on this earth was here at the creation of our planet. It was, however, in a different form. Over millennia it has been transformed through various energy reallocation and the continuing circle of life. Witnessing this conversion of energy demonstrates many concepts including that we are all one, all connected, and all responsible for working together with nature. Let's help with this energy transformation, one of nature's brilliant plans, and support the cycle of life into the bargain.

  - utilise children's paintings and drawings as cards and wrapping paper
  - find someone with a compost system, worm farm or hungry chickens to give your food scraps to (no citrus for worms or chickens please).

- **Trip to the tip.** Go together to a local landfill to show children – and remind yourself! – how large an area it is. Discuss why it's important to put less in these landfills and repair, reuse and recycle more.

- **Sort it out.** Sort recycling with children. Check a recycling chart or find out other ways to recycle waste in your area. Separate and wash any recyclable items. If you have kerbside collection, store the items ready for the next pick up. If not, have them available next time you're going past the large recycling bins in your community.

- **Break it down.** Create and use home recycling options such as a compost system or worm farm. Children can assist in all stages of this and learn to separate their own additions. Discuss what happens to the food in the compost heap or worm farm and find out how it can be used on yours or others' gardens to feed the plants.

Where do I fit in?

We are all part of a family. We all have ancestors (tīpuna or tūpuna) and a lineage (whakapapa) extending through generations. Even if we cannot specify the exact path or know anything about them, our ancestral links are very much a part of who we are today.

Some of us are members of blended families. Children are often fascinated as to who is connected to whom and why they are no longer connected. How come they share a grandparent with me but they have different parents? Tell me again? It can be a little like putting together a familial jigsaw puzzle.

In many cultures, knowing the family lineage in detail and understanding when, where and why major events in our history happened, forms the basis of who we are. From generation to generation, our ancestors' experiences have been passed down to us through genetics as well as through the sharing of knowledge, skills, stories and wisdom. When staying on marae, the very walls and ceilings are supported by the tīpuna or tūpuna of the tangata whenua (people of the land) who watch over us during our sleep in the wharenui (main house).

We may descend from many different ethnic backgrounds. These collective cultural threads form a special part of who we are. More so if we acknowledge, appreciate and seek out further understanding about these ancestral links.

There are many questions to be asked about our whakapapa and some answers may remain elusive. Who came before us? What did they experience during their lives? How has this shaped how I live my life now? What is important about where and how I live now and how does this link to my ancestors? How can I discover more about – and reconnect with – my past lineage? These may be some of the questions that spark children's interest in their family history.

The family had been separated and re-combined as many families have these days. The grandchildren were trying to figure it all out one evening. "So, you're married to Namie now, Papa, but you used to be married to Mama and Mama is now married to Pip." "Correct." "And you're Mum's Dad and Mama is Mum's Mum." "That's right." "I think you and Mama should be married again." "Oh, really? But what about Namie?" "Well, Namie could die ...." one suggested. Luckily, Namie is understanding about the ways children view the world!

Everyone is part of the story of the world. We each have a right to recognise our thread in the magnificent, multi-dimensional tapestry of life.

Experience this ...

- **Family talk.** Talk together about what you know about your families. How far back in history can you discuss?

- **Building family knowledge.** Ask those who may know more than you – perhaps older relatives – to build up your understanding of your family histories.

- **Family tree.** Create a family tree together: draw, write, paint, gather and stick in photos or create a special song to sing about your family's journey through generations.

- **Pictures and stories.** Prepare drawn or photographed pictures and stories of important people in your lives. Perhaps recount recent adventures you've had together or family events you've attended.

- **Pass them on.** Find out about family stories – both recent and old – and retell them often to help you remember them and pass them on. Perhaps make a family book of the stories together.

- **Where did you come from?** Discover other ways of describing who you are and where you come from. You could create a 'pepeha,' to state significant family history landmarks through to the names of those you are most recently descended from and connected to.

- **Family learning.** Learn together about the local, regional and national history of where you have come from as well as where you currently live. Te Tiriti O Waitangi (Treaty of Waitangi) is important to understand for everyone connected with Aotearoa New Zealand. The late Bishop Manu Bennett referred to the Treaty as, "the promise of two peoples to take the best possible care of each other."

- **Cultural groups.** Seek out cultural groups that are relevant to elements of your lineage. An example is the Shetland Society of Wellington. There are many other local European, Pacific, African or Asian groups or societies. Find, join and support them.

Loving **beautiful** bodies

Children are naturally inquisitive and proud of their bodies. As babies, we all gazed up in wonder at our inexplicably turning hands. We discovered that we could reach our toes and suck them. Poking our tummy button was rather entertaining and genitals provided much interest. Through the years, testing out the limits of what we could actually do with this body of ours – let's face it – was just downright, overwhelmingly, jump-up-and-down fantastic!

Allowing children to explore and feel confident in their bodies – and ensuring that they know their bodies are their own to be pleased with – is critical in ensuring children grow up self-assured in this 'body image focused' society. However, any issues that we have about our own body may be inadvertently modelled and potentially influence children's learning. Implicit acceptance of nakedness and positive reinforcement about our own and children's bodies sends them the message that bodies are okay. Or even better, that bodies are really quite marvellous.

As with all labelling of people, we must be wary of the ripple effects it can cause. Girls who are often told they look pretty may continually strive to be 'pretty' to meet this expectation. Likewise, boys who are praised for their 'manly' muscles may struggle later on with the reality of their lanky or smaller-than-hoped-for body.

This 'failing' can contribute to a life-long insecurity about their body. Avoiding such labelling is important; even those labels we perceive as positive.

Our children are perfect just the way they are. There is nothing rude, naughty, evil, ugly, disgusting or offensive about anything to do with their bodies. When referring to nakedness, it is worth going to lengths to avoid the use of any of these or similar words. Let's support our children to love their bodies in the way their early instincts have inspired them to do.

> Some statements used by children:
> "When I see someone naked, I don't laugh." "Mummy, can I please kiss your beautiful yummy gummy body?"

Once we love and appreciate our own physical form, we have a greater chance of being able to appreciate others for who they are.

Experience this ...

- **Show respect.** Consider how you view your own body or the bodies of others. How do you speak about bodies? Could you use different language to ensure you are demonstrating respect for the human form in all its varieties?

- **Gently does it.** Slow down physical interactions with your own or anybody else's body and treat them with kindness, respect and even reverence.

- **Get naked.** Take a moment the next time you have a bath or shower or get changed to notice your nakedness. If you feel comfortable with children seeing you naked and it is appropriate for them to do so, this can be a lovely opportunity for modelling confidence in – and appreciation for – your body. Go about your naked business without making a big deal of it.

- **Sing a song, dance a jig.** Create a special song or dance you can do together when children or you are naked (again, as appropriate). Celebrate this freedom and encourage delight in bodies.

- **All bodies great and small.** Find books or songs or talk about people of all sorts of shaped and sized bodies: tall as a house, short as a mushroom, round like a pudding, thin like a carrot. Discuss how all these varieties are beautiful. How boring this world would be if we're all shaped the same. It's also good to model respectful language when talking about different body shapes.

If children are doing something to your body that you don't like, let them know you don't like it and request that they stop. Also stop whenever they request you to do so.

Nakedness of adults around children and vice versa is often not seen as a good thing. However, how better to show them what real bodies look like? How better to affirm children's bodies as beautiful? The key to ensuring everyone's safety is mutual respect. This must be modelled first by the adults and will later be granted by children.

Worryingly, the female form is continually misrepresented in the media and in day-to-day life. Popular dolls and cartoon characters over-emphasise particular characteristics of the female body and are, in reality, anatomically impossible. Girls are bombarded by 'Photoshopped' fashion models in the media creating unrealistic role models. This bombardment can culminate in later attempts to meet these unattainable goals. This misrepresentation can also cloud others' expectations, further adding pressure for girls to look this unrealistic way.

Little drops of life

Water is the essence of life. We drink it, swim in it, play in it, wash in it, listen to it, watch it, experiment with it, love it, and live with it. Without water there would be no life as we know it. Evolution began in the water and most living things are predominantly made up of water. A human body is made up from 50-75 per cent water. We were nurtured to full term within a water-filled pouch. The sound of running water or the feel of warm water are among the more calming of life's experiences. There are few children who are not totally drawn to a sink or bucket of water with which they may while away hours playing and – even better – being in it.

When frozen, water solidifies as ice. When heated to a high enough temperature, it becomes steam. Both can be soothing and healing for our bodies. I was recently reminded of its power to heal when I overheard a four year old telling his Mum, who had complained of a headache and tired body, "Water makes you feel better." He is right: a healthy body is also a hydrated body.

One Saturday it started to pour down. She asked, "Who'd like to dance with me in the rain?" One took her up on the offer and they had a wonderfully invigorating experience. Holding hands, they twirled around, their faces up to the heavens; dramatic, free and beautiful. Back inside, they warmed their chilly toes together, their feet in a little bath, towels wrapped around them, eyes still wide and sparkling. Magic!

Drinkable water – and in the ideal world, all fresh water would be drinkable – is the best drink we can give our bodies. There are no added sugars, colours or flavours to pollute our delicate forms. Our bodies process water beautifully and use it to flush harmful toxins from our system.

Unfortunately, water is becoming scarce in more countries due to pollution and wasteful usage. It therefore requires us to be respectful of its use. Conscious respect and appreciation of our local water supply can provide us with fun, learning, health and happiness. Get drinking! Get wet!

Experience this ...

- **Bottle it.** Carry around drink bottles for you and children to sip from regularly during the day. Make it a habit.

- **Easy access**. Provide children with easy access to drinking water so they can help themselves.

- **Puddle play.** Allow children to play in puddles when the idea takes them. Even better, have a go yourself!

- **Water talk.** Talk about why we need to conserve water. Model careful use of water: leave a bucket in the sink or shower to catch drips and waste water for use on the garden; have small baths and short showers using an egg-timer or other alarm. Save the planet one drop at a time.

- **Clean play.** Create water play while cleaning bodies in a paddling pool, bath or bucket. Pour water with cups or leaves; create a fountain or cycle the water around the container.

Respect for water, and having an understanding of its preciousness for all living things, is critical to our survival and that of our planet.

- **Rain dance.** Utilise the opportunities of rain showers and puddles for water play. Dancing in the rain is the best!

- **Wishy-washy.** Make it possible for children to do the dishes or hand wash clothes. It's a great opportunity to play respectfully with water.

- **Water quest.** Together, discuss where water comes from. Talk about the water cycle in general as well as your local water supply's journey to your tap. Can you visit some of the sites along this journey?

- **Water potions.** What drinkable potions and teas can you create with water?

- **Watering life.** Carefully water garden areas and talk about the need plants have to drink water. Give pets their water. Again, talk with children about the importance of water for the health and well-being of all living things.

- **Go forth.** Visit a spring, stream, river or lake and discuss the benefits to the earth of this fresh water. If the water is safe to drink directly from the source, this can be an unforgettably satisfying experience. Discussions of how water flows through all of us and keeps us healthy can conclude a memorable expedition.

- **Sea visit.** Discuss the difference between sea water and fresh water. Boil or freeze some seawater. Have a little taste. What benefits can sea water provide over fresh water and vice versa?

Pay it forward

Kindness is defined in the Oxford Dictionary as: "The quality of being friendly, generous and considerate." When we combine this quality with empathy – the ability to identify with and understand somebody else's feelings or difficulties – we have harnessed a powerful combination of human traits that can greatly enhance the lives of ourselves and others.

Introducing a nine year old to the concept of Timebanking: "It's where everyone's time is valuable and we use our own skills to help other people who haven't got those skills or don't want to do those jobs. So maybe you could do some things for people like walking their dogs after school or making them a cake." "And someone else could clean up my room," he added with a sly grin.

Her second child was very young, didn't sleep much at night and was very needy during the day. She also had a one year old to care for and the house to keep somewhat in order. One day her neighbour popped in to bring them their post. She saw the young mother's grey pallor and the desperation in her eyes. Then she spotted the clothes basket. "I'll take that," she said. Outside she went to hang the washed clothes on the line. Later that day she arrived with a meal for the family. Oh, the sense of relief and gratitude!

Evidence shows that helping others can reduce stress as well as improve our mood, self-esteem and happiness. I'm sure we could all do with some of that.

Each of us has our own life experiences. These experiences reflect the ebb and flow of our lives as we encounter various situations and journey through different life stages. There are times when we need help and times when we are more able to help others. Whether we generate or receive acts of kindness, we are participating in the 'pay it forward' process, supporting the interdependence of the human species.

Children need to see and experience this process in action so that they can participate in it themselves. They need to appreciate the benefits of demonstrating kindness to other people through conscious actions. For this reason, it's important for children to observe adults graciously acknowledging and accepting help from others.

Thinking back, how many times has somebody done something kind for you which has caused you to consider your next encounter? It may have been letting you into a stream of heavy traffic or giving you back something you hadn't noticed you'd dropped.

Kindness can be expressed in many ways. It may be a few kind words; helping a neighbour weed their garden or helping out at a homeless shelter. It can also be modelled in day-to-day interactions with children and others, both strangers and those we know well. Who will be your next recipient?

By carrying out an act of kindness for another person, we participate in the interdependence process human beings rely on for survival. We are empathically offering our services without need of repayment, knowing that helping others helps us all.

Experience this ...

- **Empathy.** With children, acknowledge – in simple terms – other peoples' current life situations. Empathise, asking what life might be like for them. When you see there is need, ask, "What can we do to help?" Do those things that inspire both you and the children. These might include visiting, doing household jobs, making a gift or an invitation to a meal or some other fun event.

- **Accept kindness.** Consider how you respond to offers of help. Do you gratefully accept? Or do you habitually say, "No, I'm alright," and then later think that perhaps it would have been great to accept? If so, practice pausing before responding to kind offers. Next time a helping hand is extended try saying, "Yes" whether or not you feel you need the assistance. Let children know what help you've accepted lately.

- **Notice, recognise, respond.** Acknowledge children verbally when they carry out acts of kindness for you or for others: "That was very kind of you to share your toy with your little brother" or "I really appreciated your kind help laying the table just now."

- **Plus one.** Together, choose an extra grocery item on a regular basis and donate it a local food-bank. Explain how this helps other people in your community.

- **RAK.** Carry out random acts of kindness, for anyone, at any time. These can be spontaneous or planned by you. The idea is that the receiver is not expecting this kind action. Keep on the lookout for opportunities for kindness and you may even surprise yourself. Set a goal of doing one each week or even one each day.

Pay it forward can be extended to pets, creatures and other living things. Household pets and local birds and insects provide a wonder-full opportunity for practicing expressing kindness and experiencing the personal benefits of helping life flourish. Encouraging a culture of kindness in everything we do supports children to grow up valuing this necessary human trait.

Pay it forward is about both giving and receiving. We do something for someone and they do something for someone else and so on. At a later point, something is done for us. Sometimes we need to create structure around this and practice until it becomes, 'just what we do'.

- **Give a little.** Support children to choose clothes and toys to give away to those they know; to opportunity shops or to agencies that support others in need such as Women's Refuge.

- **Cooking with kindness.** Make meals together and take them to those who you know are in need. Consider those with sickness in the family; a new baby and mother enjoying their 'babymoon' or someone who lives alone and would relish some company.

- **Volunteer.** Consider what volunteer work you do or could be involved in? Perhaps church, school, sports, refugee centre, marae, activities, or causes you believe in. Involve children in this work. What assistance could they give you? What's appropriate for them to be included in?

G-o-o-o-o-o-o s-l-o-o-o-o-w

When we slow our frenetic pace, taking a few moments to be silent; to breathe and simply look around us, we may notice how much more we appreciate and take in our surroundings. Consider the colour of a ladybird's wings; the sound of a cicada or the smell of a newborn baby.

During these times, we also have an opportunity to reconnect our minds with our bodies; to check where we are at physically and emotionally. We can even become more effective at accomplishing everyday tasks when we slow our thoughts and movements and take time to consider the beauty and satisfaction derived from the careful journey through a particular task. This is part of the practice of 'mindfulness'. From the peace of mindfulness, insights can arise. Insights are the sparks of life's learning.

We can begin to experience mindfulness by choosing to simply s-l-o-w d-o-w-n. Children often enjoy the novelty of moving and talking in slow motion. This 'go slow' practice can eventually include the slowing of thoughts as well. By turning off our auto-pilot, we can focus on each thought so that each action can be consciously chosen and undertaken.

They decided to have a four-generation trip to visit relatives who lived about six hours away. Two children under three, along with their mother, grandmother and great-grandfather (aged 90) all packed into one van! Other family members said it was mad to take so many dependent people. But they found that in moving at the pace of the 90 year old, they were also moving at the pace of the very young ones. No rushing.

There were many loo stops and short walks whenever the van doors opened. Lots of singing in the van, lots of marvelling at points of shared interest and tiny adventures.

Even a tear or two as the very young took the hand of the very old to explore. The journey took way longer than six hours, but how they travelled was far more memorable than what they did when they got there.

Slow, silent, and conscious moments allow a space for peace, love and creativity to be opened up. These gifts of consciousness can be quietly dispersed to the world.

Experience this ...

- **Slow it right down.** Do your next task in slow motion, with or without children.

- **Time for tasks.** Make lunch, do the dishes, or talk to each other in slow motion. Discover which tasks work better in slow motion and which ones need speed and momentum for success.

- **Schedule slow.** Schedule a 'go slow' time together. Undertake tasks during this time with careful focus. Work through them step-by-step. Take satisfaction in both the journey and completion. Laugh and enjoy the novelty together. Let the time unfold however it does. Talk about the reasons for trying this experiment and discuss how it went afterwards.

Make sure that you don't have any major pressures during the 'go slow' times and have fairly quick foods available so that you do not have to 'go slow' over preparations for an elaborate menu if you're hungry.

- **Downtime, together time.** Ensure regular 'go slow' time is shared together, mindfully, enjoying each other's company.

- **Make it last.** Extend the time you 'go slow' to stretch out to an hour or two or even a whole day.

Amazing **moves**

L ove of movement and confidence in how our bodies move can be with us throughout our lives. The earlier children are provided with opportunities to experiment with their body movements, the stronger the foundations of this love and confidence will be.

"Putting babies into any position that they cannot get into or out of by themselves is helplessness training …," writes Pennie Brownlee in "Dance with me in the Heart." Ideally, babies will spend much of their free time each day lying on their backs working on the basics of how their bodies move. Controlling newborn reflexes; building up their core muscles; balancing out their bodies; learning to roll, crawl, sit, stand and finally, the moment everyone's waiting for: they learn to walk by themselves.

Some great news is that adults can easily nurture learning about movement without needing to teach babies to move or buy things to help them move. Time, a blanket and a flat, warm space is the only equipment needed for babies to learn their own natural movement. They will do a beautiful job all on their own. The side effects include developing a sense of control over their lives and the self confidence that only comes through persistence and achieving something for ourselves.

For older children, skipping; forward rolls; handstands with feet up a wall and walking along the sea wall or on top of a low flat wall are all beneficial to children's poise and self-belief. Rolling down a grassy bank; walking along lines on the pavement; tippy toe steps and learning to hop all provide movement magic for littlies and biggies alike. What were the movements that made our smiles wide with excitement and cheeks flushed with achievement as children? Leapfrog over friends, posts or stools? Rolling about on the grass or on pillows? Riding ramps on bikes or skates? Hops, skips and jumps? How high could we jump? How long? What happened when we tried to stand on our hands? How did we pretend to fly?

We can use household objects and furniture to create wonderful challenges with children. Many items make great boundaries to run, move or cycle around. Chalked foot and hand prints show where to aim our feet and hands. Chalk lines or cracks in the pavement can be followed on tippy toes. A wind chime can be jumped up to and tapped.

The seven month old baby had never been put into a sitting position. She was always laid on her back. From there she had taught herself to roll onto her front, then back again, and later rolling over and over and pivoting to get to wherever she wanted. One day her family were sitting on the couch, talking. The baby was practicing her moves on the floor. Suddenly they heard a delightful burble and looked up to see her sitting on her bottom, absolutely beaming! She had done it! She had done it herself! She had worked out how to roll onto her tummy, push up on hands and knees and then tilt sideways until she was sitting on her own. No chance of falling backwards and cracking her head; she was totally safe. She could get into and out of that sitting position all by herself. What a sense of achievement she just experienced!

If I can move my own body as I wish, imagine what I can do to contribute to our world!

Blankets thrown over low or high chairs make tunnels to wriggle through. Wooden planks, stones and leaf paths all add interest.

When we look around, we can find the fun inside and outside to help keep children moving and we might even want to have a go ourselves!

Experience this ...

- **Move it.** Think and talk about movement you remember doing as a child. Did you often walk to school or the dairy? Where was the best place to run hard and fast? Consider similarities and differences to what physical activities children do now.

- **Watch and wait.** Observe children's movements without interfering. Young babies provide many interesting poses for you to be amazed at. Can you copy them?

- **Give them space.** Allow children as much control and freedom of their body movements as possible, whatever their current stage of development. 'Less is more' for achieving this goal. No flashy equipment is required. Floor space, a grassy area, stairs, furniture, and household items can be used for the practice and development of most movements. Allow plenty of time. Assess risk together and be available in case children hurt themselves or need reassurance.

- **Walk like an elephant.** Have fun with basic movements together. Do funny walking and movements with children: holding hands, backwards, sideways, high and low, jumps, knees and crawls, with a book on your heads, blindfolded or eyes closed.

Children's movements change as their bodies and perspectives grow and develop. Noticing this can help us to understand and perhaps support their current developmental stage.

'Nappy off' time is helpful for supporting young babies to experience what movements their bodies can do.

- **Getting over obstacles.** Create obstacle courses together. Follow children's lead and use, "Okay, let's try it," in abundance. Make courses inside and out of doors. Have a go at these with children to experience the joy of what bodies can do and have a laugh together.

Little places to call our own

In this world full of people and things, it can sometimes be difficult to find any sanctuary for ourselves. Creatively finding little places to call our own – even when space is limited – can allow us a refuge from the daily goings-on; a place where we can breathe out and feel safe.

Children often like to hide things. To keep them safe; keep them hidden; curled up tight to be discovered and unfurled at another time. We may never know why, but squirrelling away a shell ring or fork-like twig, an old sock, a dead spider, or a secret key may be a way of children expressing themselves or be part of their process of making sense of their world.

Feeling that they have a little bit of control over their environment is perhaps one side effect. Keeping some secret treasure that no-one else knows about and having one thing or place to call their own is also part of children's growing independence. Their secret treasure hoard may be representative of their life experience and an expression of their free will. In any case, secret spaces for children to call their own are worthy of our respect.

Just as treasure boxes are a wonderful way to keep cherished items safe from harm sometimes it is the children themselves who wish to be curled up, safe and secure. It could be on a special chair; in a hidey-hole nest of blankets or boxes; a comfy cushion or beanbag; a secret cupboard or a spongy, grassy, sunny spot outside. It could be the gap behind the door, under the table, or the space beneath Grandma's open umbrella. Imagine a storyteller's cave; a clandestine games closet; an outside playhouse or any other special space to rest, contemplate or play out their current experience of life. All these safe and 'hidden' places can support children – as well as adults – in feeling secure and confident about their place in this world.

A young child used both transporting (moving things) and enveloping (hiding things) schemas to make sense of the world. Together they made a 'nest' behind the couch with cushions and blankets, partly so that Dad would at least know where his wallet and phone were when they inexplicably disappeared!

We can trust in the world and our right to be here when we know we are safe, and that those things we treasure are also safe.

Experience this ...

- **Your own little corner in the world.** Consider what provisions you have for your own space and things. What areas feel sacred for you? How do you feel when you are there or using that area? If you do not have such a place – a chair, spot in the garden, under a tree, or on the floor by a bottom drawer – perhaps create one.

- **A box to call your own.** Together, find a box or container in which children can store their treasures. Acknowledge that it is theirs to do with as they wish and that you will respect it and help protect it from harm.

- **A space to call your own.** Notice if children already have some areas around the house to which they gravitate regularly and where they appear totally comfortable. Safe havens in times of necessity or fun and space for alone time. If so, ensure these areas are respected when the children wish to use them. If it's an awkward spot for others, help them to find another.

- **Hut time.** Create a hut together for all of you to play in. Use everyday items around the house and have children take the lead whenever possible. Follow their requests and instructions and help them to learn from their mistakes by allowing real life consequences to happen. Discuss alternatives for next time.

- **Make a nest.** Find or create a space that children can use as a nest when they wish. A tiny, snuggly spot could be used as a gathering point for the day's treasures or a place to curl up in. Smaller is usually better: a cosy gap between sofa and wall or the doorstep.

- **Story spot.** Create special places to tell stories, do puzzles or crafts, lie down and rest, talk about your day, role play, re-enact life and whatever else you wish to do in a snug, safe environment, together or alone. Let children decorate or lay these out as they wish each time.

Knowing where children hide things – including themselves - can be helpful when looking for those lost keys or when you suddenly notice a strangely silent house.

If children share a room, it's helpful to provide each with a little space for themselves and their treasures. Hanging fabric can easily cordon off a special space.

Special places outside of home may be appreciated for their transient nature. Huddle beneath a tree at a park while sitting on a familiar blanket or with it draped over the lower branches.

Embracing **body functions**

We've all got one, but only one: our body. It's crucial we know how to assess and care for it so as to help maximise our journey through this life. It's never too early to begin talking with children about the basics of maintaining bodily health. Indeed, those living with young children may have discovered that the locked toilet door has become a thing of the past anyway and they've no choice but to answer the inevitable questions.

It is also pertinent to discuss the consequences of not caring for our body. The conscious practices that nurture our own bodies are important life skills. They lead to delight in our own unique, beautiful self and maximise our health and well-being.

Answering children's questions in a matter of fact way, using correct anatomical vocabulary, is important, particularly when these are to do with their genitals and bottom. Hearing this information without judgement or sensationalism is also a wonderful gift to help children come to an understanding and acceptance of all their body bits. It can assist them in feeling confident and respectful of their body as a whole and feeling that same way towards the bodies of others. Learning about how our bodies work and what's in store as we age, helps us to further appreciate our amazing organic machine. Learning empowers us to care for ourselves more effectively. It can also quench some nagging questions or calm an unsettling imagining of what we think our body looks like to others or how it is supposed to act.

Poos, wees, blood and mucus are produced by our bodies and when analysed, can protect our health. This analysis is a natural and sensible act to model for children. It can enable them – to a certain extent – to monitor their own physical condition. Other information about our inner health or responses to external situations is constantly being processed and communicated by our bodies. Listening to what our body is letting us know is worthy of our attention. Open the door, my friends, and wait for the wonder-full questioning to begin!

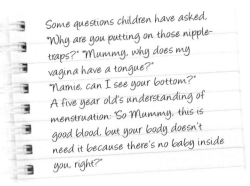

Some questions children have asked.
"Why are you putting on those nipple-traps?" "Mummy, why does my vagina have a tongue?"
"Namie, can I see your bottom?"
A five year old's understanding of menstruation: "So Mummy, this is good blood, but your body doesn't need it because there's no baby inside you, right?"

Being able to care for others and our world begins with building an understanding about caring for ourselves.

Experience this ...

• **I can do this with that.** Practice isolating and manipulating individual body parts. Our human bodies are to be utilised and each part has its own discrete and interlinked functions. This could be used as a night-time meditation; a quiet time together or even an exercise around the dining table with you all sitting there, squeezing your lower abdominal muscles or wiggling your big toes.

• **Caring for our bodies.** Engage with children from birth, about what you are doing with your own self-care routines. Use singing, drawing, acting or simply narrating while you carry these out. Respond clearly, simply and factually to their questions. All their questions are worthy of the best, most genuine response you can give them.

• **Flushing out information.** If young children wish to ask questions while you're toileting, have a go at not letting stage fright put you off your job. Instead, focus on answering their questions as pragmatically and honestly as possible. Show them whatever they wish to see: this may involve lifting your comfort levels somewhat.

• **Take a good look.** Offer interest in how children are toileting. If they wish you to see what they've done, you can simply look and comment on the health or otherwise of their deposit. Describe what you see and talk about what healthy poos and wees look like.

• **Joking.** Toilet humour can be lots of fun. Children often get right into it and are keen to talk about their poo as if it is a friend. Relax and enjoy the moment of amusement and lack of decorum. Perhaps you can make up songs or stories involving human body functions.

Puberty brings many changes for children, both physically and emotionally. The door may not be so freely open but we can offer our services and continue to provide honest and judgement-free support for them during this time.

This is just the beginning

I find parenting my three girls to be both the best and hardest job in the world. I'm challenged every day as I attempt to effectively meet their needs as well as creating other dreams, and carrying out daily demands and responsibilities. While doing this, I am trying to be conscious of my thoughts, feelings and actions. Sometimes it all turns to custard: actually, this happens fairly regularly.

I remember years ago noting with horror that my two year old's lament of, "I just can't do it. This is too hard for me!" reflected my own words, tone and expression. Over the last decade, I've learnt more than I thought possible about children and have quickly grown to appreciate the time I spend with them. But, despite all this learning and experience, I still struggle to get through the day without losing my temper in some way and flicking onto 'auto-pilot'.

It can be really hard being a parent in this society full of seemingly self-reliant, nuclear families. Many grandparents are working full-time or living elsewhere and 'everyone and their dog' is telling us what we are supposed to be doing. Even those families which hook into supportive and informative communities and networks can find the realities of modern-day parenting difficult.

However, all is not lost.

The realisation that I didn't have to do anything special to help my children's development was a light-bulb moment for me. I discovered children could join in with most daily tasks and together we could make them fun. My next shift in understanding was that doing these everyday, real life things was actually beneficial to children. I must say that with the odd breakfast-in-bed and other culinary delights appearing, I'm now reaping the benefits of my children knowing their way around the kitchen. Sure, with children, the jobs tend to take longer and often they don't work out but that's life, isn't it? Try, try and try again; adjust and try again. I endeavour to live by this quote:

"Success is the ability to go from one failure to another without loss of enthusiasm."

- Winston Churchill

Every day, I have an opportunity to try again; to clear the canvas and start afresh. In fact, every moment presents a new opportunity to have another go. Moment to moment, this is a challenge I set myself: "What's needed in this moment?" It might be that I need to take myself away to calm down or that I need to hug a seemingly 'unhuggable' child. It might be that I recognise an opportunity to stop; to notice my breath; to close my eyes and simply be alive. In the flurry of modern living, this momentary pause can make all the difference.

Writing this book has, for me, been a journey of discovery and wonder at the real benefits child's play offers all of us. This wonder-full and on-going journey has also affirmed that what I'm doing most of the time with my children is just fine, give or take a few frustrated outbursts each day. I now recognise that each positive interaction is making a positive difference in the world. Throughout this parenting adventure, I've also gathered many more ideas for change-making ways to play with children – but they will have to wait for the next book.

So, go forth and play! Play with love; play with life and give yourselves a pat on the back for what you are doing: for yourselves, for children and for our world.

Arohanui,
Sarah x

Good reads and references

Acknowledgements: Maurice Sendak
In The Night Kitchen Harper Collins 1970

Introduction: *www.māori.cl/Proverbs.htm*
by Woodward Maori, updated 5/2/14

Introduction: Dean Radin *The Noetic Universe*
Transworld Publishers 2009

Loving communication: *Mirror neurons introduction*
http://www.brainfacts.org/brain-basics/
neuroanatomy/articles/2008/mirror-neurons/
by Susan Perry 20/2/13

Loving communication: Adele Faber & Elaine
Mazlish *How To Talk So Kids Will Listen And
Listen So Kids Will Talk* Piccadilly Press Ltd 2001

Cooking for life and love: Jamie Oliver
Jamie At Home Penguin Group 2007

Cooking for life and love: Barbara Kingsolver
Animal, Vegetable, Miracle HarperPerennial 2008

The world in song: Time Magazine article
http://ideas.time.com/2013/08/16/singing-
changes-your-brain/ by Stacy Horn 16/8/13

The world in song: *Understanding hormones that
help us learn* http://crackingthelearningcode.
com/element19.html by JW Wilson, Advanced
Learning Institute 2009

Where do I fit in? Bishop Manuhuia Bennett.
Quote in Te Roroa Report to the Waitangi Tribunal
(New Zealand/1992) p8 https://forms.justice.govt.
nz/search/Documents/WT/wt_DOC_68462675/
Wai38.pdf

Pay it forward: *Helping others helps us*
http://www.mentalhealth.org.uk/help-
information/mental-health-a-z/A/altruisim/
by Mental Health Foundation

Pay it forward: http://www.timebank.org.nz/

G-o-o-o-o-o-o s-l-o-o-o-w: Dr Libby Weaver
Rushing Woman's Syndrome
Little Green Frog Publishing 2012

Amazing moves: Pennie Brownlee
Dance With Me In The Heart Playcentre
Publications 2008

Amazing moves: Mariane Hermsen-Van Wanrooy
Baby Moves Baby Moves Publications 2006

Little places to call our own: Nikolien van Wijk
Getting Started With Schemas
Playcentre Publications 2009

All URLs checked 3 March 2015.

Acknowledgements

This book has been a long time in the brewing. Many have inspired my thinking and motivated my search for further understanding. First off I thank my parents, Cheryl Amys and Peter Glensor, and my captivating Grandma, Amy Viti Olds, for influencing my positive early brain development and modelling for me the importance of community, of supporting others and standing up for my beliefs.

A big kia ora to Bronwen Olds for telling me to "go up the hill to the Playcentre, they'll look after you." You started me off on my journey of parenting discovery. To all those who I've encountered during my eight years at Playcentre. Thank you for all your support, encouragement, inspiration and aroha. And to the Playcentre movement in general, there really is no more effective and supportive way in New Zealand (or the world!) to grow as a parent and enjoy children's early years. I bow to you in thanks and most grateful acknowledgement.

I must impart appreciation to Landmark Education whose courses first challenged me to consider the importance of how I was giving and receiving communication. I discovered the power I have to take responsibility for choices I make and my impacts on the world. As a teen I was also inspired by Michael Jackson's songs calling on me to make a difference.

I extend heartfelt gratitude to the many wise and wonder-full wāhine I'm privileged enough to know and love. We have shared many a cuppa or meal, or played with our tamariki, while discussing what these burgeoning understandings and beliefs are all about. Along with discussing the inherent challenges, with these ideas sometimes running perpendicular, or even completely opposite, to popular parenting methods. In particular, thanks to Annemarie, Barb, Karen, Kena, Jane, Sarah and Sue for your direct assistance with the completion of this book and the launch of www.childrenchange.co.nz. Kia ora te whānau for helping me get many of the photographs for this book and my future use, and for encouraging me on this exciting adventure.

I have greatly appreciated the decision of Brainwave Trust Aotearoa to take me on as a Kaiako (Educator), even though I was initially something of a 'dark horse'. My knowledge and confidence in the 'Early Years' messages has been strengthened enormously through doing this work that I love. Kathryn, thanks so much for your early belief in me, and to Nathan and Miriam, particularly, for doing the incredible work you do and being willing to scoop me up for the ride. It is an honour. To the rest of the Brainwave team, you are truly an inspiration. What a massive difference you are all making to the health and wellbeing of Aotearoa New Zealand.

To Ako books – Playcentre Publications Limited, particularly Ginny, Maree, Melanie and Morna. Thank you for recognising the importance of the messages I wish to communicate, offering me this opportunity to publish my first book and supporting my journey over this last year. Here's to many more! Vicki, my esteemed editor, thank you for sharing your expertise in book creation with me over many a Skype call and email. I greatly appreciated the gifts of your 'devil's advocate' questioning and the acknowledgement of your own learning throughout our editing journey together, as we "kneaded and punched it and pounded and pulled … till it looked okay."

Thank you to Pennie Brownlee for the brave and true points you are making about how we view and treat children in our culture. I appreciate the challenges and gifts you offer. You've been my hero for many years.

Appreciation must be extended to the many people from whom I gleaned change-making ideas and experiences, through kōrero or observing them in action. Many of which feature in this book. Of particular note are Annika (Germany) for the pizza massages and Cate (Australia) for, "Stop, calm, do no harm," which my five year old now uses to great effect.

To my glorious girls – Lucy, Sophie, and Kendra – and to all of the tamariki I've had the pleasure of interacting with at Playcentre, school, at various events and places. It is from you that most of the gold in this book has originated. You have re-taught me about play, the freedom of having fun, slowing down and appreciating the joy of the moment ("Mum, you're being a 'rushing woman' again"), and demonstrated the wisdom and huge capabilities of babies and children. Kia ora, kia ora, kia ora! It is you all who have inspired me more than any to strive to be the best parent (and person) I can be, and to encourage others to do the same.

Richard, my husband, my number one fan, my rock. I acknowledge your openness and love for me and my, sometimes 'over the rainbow', ideas. When times are good you are the wind beneath my wings. When times are difficult you remind me of the importance of caring for myself and my family foremost.

Kia ora koutou! You have all had a hand in creating who I am today and pointing me in this exciting direction. I look forward to continued interactions with you all and many more people as we journey on, making a difference in the world with everything we think, feel and do.

Sarah Amy Glensor Best, February 2015

Sarah Amy Glensor Best is many things to many people – mum of three, Playcentre facilitator, Brainwave Trust kaiako, change activist, conscious parenting advocate, author. In Changing the World is Child's Play Sarah shares her passion in making the world a better place. It can be done. She believes the single most effective way to create positive change is through meaningful child's play. Put simply, it starts with sharing loving, real life experiences with children.

Sarah blogs, speaks and facilitates workshops on play and other parenting and childhood topics. She lives in Wellington, New Zealand with her partner and three daughters.

This is her first book and hopes that there will be opportunities for many more in the future.

Children change with every experience
Children change those around them
Children change the world
Children change the future

www.childrenchange.co.nz